WHERE DID ALL THE COWBOYS GO?

Also by Joe Millard

Seeing Through Gray Colored Lens
The Quiet Journey, Memoirs 1936 to 2000

WHERE DID ALL THE COWBOYS GO?

a memoir

JOE MILLARD

Joe Millard

iUniverse, Inc.
Bloomington

Where Did All the Cowboys Go?

Copyright © 2011 by Joe Millard

All rights reserved. No part of this book may be used or reproduced by any means, graphic, electronic, or mechanical, including photocopying, recording, taping or by any information storage retrieval system without the written permission of the author except in the case of brief quotations embodied in critical articles and reviews.

iUniverse books may be ordered through booksellers or by contacting:

iUniverse
1663 Liberty Drive
Bloomington, IN 47403
www.iuniverse.com
1-800-Authors (1-800-288-4677)

Because of the dynamic nature of the Internet, any Web addresses or links contained in this book may have changed since publication and may no longer be valid. The views expressed in this work are solely those of the author and do not necessarily reflect the views of the publisher, and the publisher hereby disclaims any responsibility for them.

Any people depicted in stock imagery provided by Thinkstock are models, and such images are being used for illustrative purposes only.

Certain stock imagery © Thinkstock.

ISBN: 978-1-4502-8313-7 (sc)
ISBN: 978-1-4502-8315-1 (dj)
ISBN: 978-1-4502-8314-4 (ebk)

Printed in the United States of America

iUniverse rev. date: 01/20/2011

For Mrs. Williams and teachers everywhere

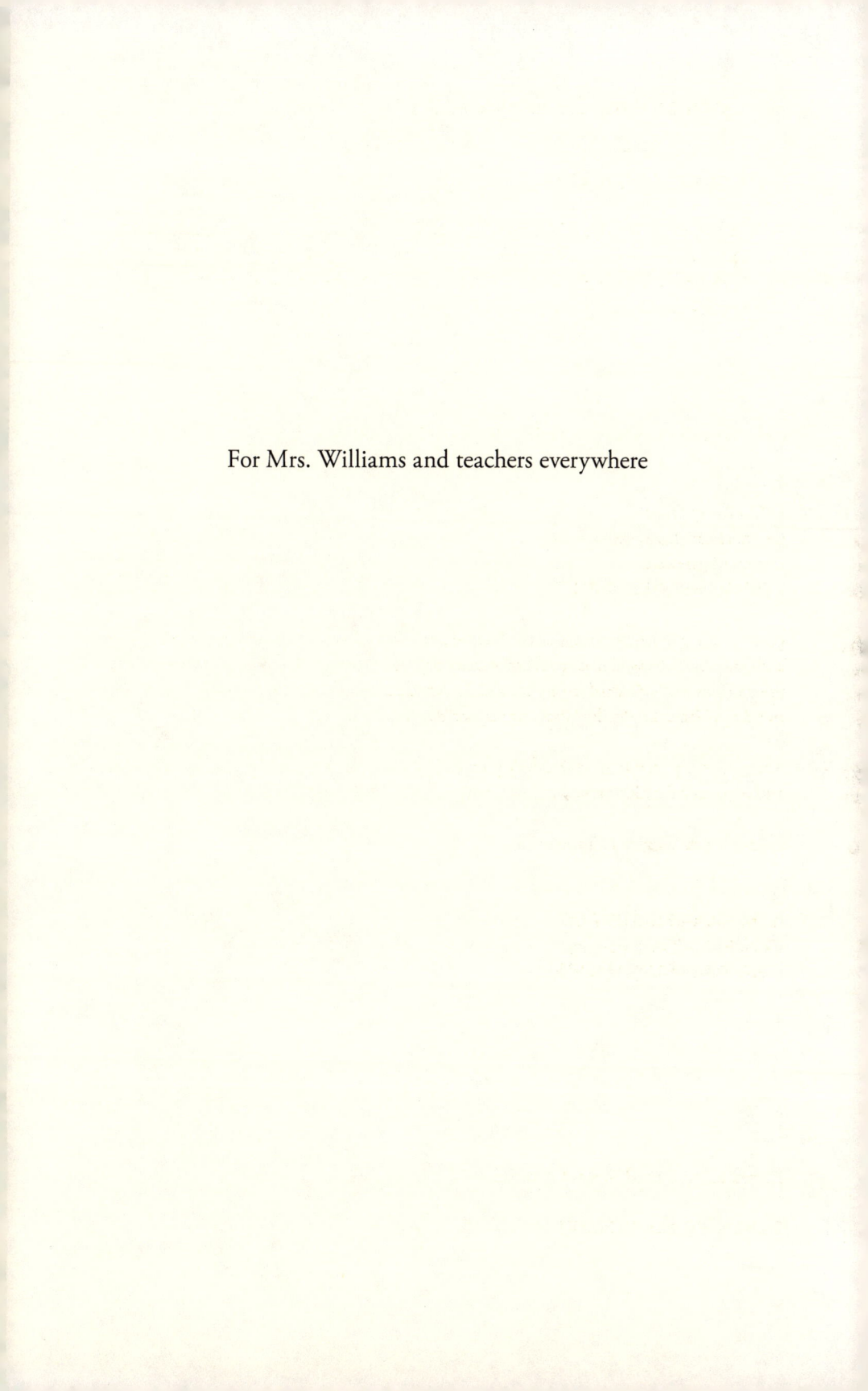

Preface

Where Did All The Cowboys Go? is about growing up on an Iowa farm in the 1940s. The book introduces teachers, neighbors, and my parents who guide and influence me consciously and subconsciously. The memoir reveals much about my one room school education, where I study geography from a globe, read the children's classics, learn sportsmanship on the play ground, and buy war bonds. The memoir also tells of my non-classroom learning experiences in Farlin, Iowa, a small rural village. It is here I learn to play pool at the village gossip center next to the blacksmith shop, loathe boxing in the IOOF hall, and understand friendship at a box social. At the Hardin Creek I learn to fish and swim, and in the farm marshlands and the surrounding hills I reenact combat scenes from Saturday war movies.

There is nothing unusual about these experiences, and my childhood is similar to the lives of thousands of children who grew up on farms in the Midwest and the Great Plains in the 1940s. Older readers, when reading these stories, will recall attending Saturday cowboy movies, participating in Christmas school plays, fishing in creeks, and enjoying community social events. Younger readers will learn that history is more than national personalities, wars, and horrible catastrophes.

This is a history book, a nonfiction book, and a memoir. To get the stories correct I have talked to relatives and friends. Sometimes we remembered differently, so I have verified events from books about one-room schools, newspaper clippings, report cards, pictures, old newspaper stories, 1940s Iowa curriculum guides, and the 1950s Iowa Eighth Grade Examination.

Where Did All The Cowboys Go? is told by Gene as best as I can remember them from September 1941 until graduating from the eighth grade in May 1950. I am the narrator describing the rural Iowa landscape, placing words in the mouths of the characters, and introducing Gene. My name was Gene throughout my childhood and adolescence.

Joe Millard

Gene's first day of school
September 1, 1941

Acknowledgements

Public education is an experiment that was made possible for me and thousands of Americans by the United States Government Land Ordinance that was written by Thomas Jefferson in 1785. The young government realized the importance of a public education and required townships to set aside land for public schools. When Iowa became a state sixty-one years later, the state legislators went further and guaranteed tuition free public schools. A tax supported public school system for educating the youth was an idea not familiar to the rest of the world. The educational experiment was a progressive initiative that helped countless young people in this country. I am indebted to this experiment.

I owe my memorable one room school experiences to dedicated teachers, a supportive community and caring parents. During the challenging 1940s while recovering from a world depression and fighting a massive world war, the educational system did not relax its responsibility to the children. I profited from those who were farsighted enough to see the importance of a good education, and who sacrificed to provide that education.

I believe it is important to share the stories about earlier years and pass them on to younger generations. Not because the stories disclose acts of great courage, or make known personal struggles, but because they reveal ordinary dreams and everyday frustrations. In these stories about growing up on an Iowa farm, I wish to convey to children today that their dreams and fears may be very similar to the dreams and fears of those who lived before them. The bigger difference is environment, and the surroundings that suggest different needs. However, beyond the surroundings and the atmosphere the basic needs are not all that much different.

Being raised on a farm in Iowa in the 1940's was as fun, scary, relaxed, stressful, peaceful, and as tense as a boy could wish for. There was space that provided freedom; and parents, teachers, family, and neighbors who protected him from himself.

The stories I tell are true and they did happen, but I have changed the names of some teachers and classmates to save them and me embarrassment. Mrs. Williams is the actual name of the teacher I had for my sixth, seventh, and eighth grades, and she was the perfect teacher for me with my many questions and need to keep busy. Mr. Morris is the name of the Greene County School Superintendent; I couldn't change the name of a county official. Every boy needs a friend like Jimmy, to find trouble with and laugh with; Jimmy is the real name of my side kick. Farlin is a real village that no longer exists except on old maps and in my mind. The people of Farlin were real people, but their names have been changed, except for Mrs. Bauman. Her home was always a safe haven for me.

I have not named my brothers or sister since I wished to focus on the relationship with my parents. I do wish to thank Dan, Jerry, Mike, and Karen for the many lessons they taught me while growing up. I have used the actual names of my uncles, aunts, and cousins. I have so many relatives that the only way to keep the stories honest is not to confuse the people, so I used their names.

I wish to thank Bill Sherman for his encouragement to write about my one room school experiences and his suggestions when I was writing, *Where Did All The Cowboys Go?* I thank Ann Hanigan for her skillful editing, and teaching me grammar that I failed to learn in the one room schools. Appreciation goes to my writing support group: Ann Boultinghouse, Carol A. Leach, Carol Tershak, Howard K. Hall, Linda

Nies, Linda Railey, and Marian Jacobs, for their patience in helping me with questions, and their help in critiquing my stories. I am especially thankful for my wife's assistance in reviewing my writing, keeping me honest, and reading my stories over and over again.

Illustration Credits

All photos, tests, and illustrations are from the author's own collection.

Following Preface Gene's first day of school September 1, 1941.

Part Two 1946-1950 Gene and Jimmy return from an unsuccessful fishing excursion.

Appendix B Iowa High School Admission Certificate

Appendix C Honor I Letter

Contents

Preface..vii
Acknowledgements.......................................ix
Illustration Credits..................................xii
1941..1
1942...21
1943...37
1944...57
1945...72

Part Two 1946 to 1950

1946...91
1947..112
1948..132
1949..153
1950..171
Epilogue..181
About The Author......................................183
Reading Club Discussion Questions.....................185
Discussion questions for young readers................187
Student Activities....................................189
References..191
Appendix A Sampling of questions from the 1950 Iowa Eight
       Grade Examination..........................195
Appendix B Iowa High School Admission Certificate.....217
Appendix C Honor I Letter.............................219

1941

Gene and his dad exit the Howard Theater and are welcomed by a gentle August breeze not often felt in Iowa. The cool wind grants instant relief from the theater's muggy air. Tonight's movie featured *Melody Ranch* starring Gene Autry. There was also a short Bugs Bunny cartoon, a Green Hornet serial, and a newsreel highlighting Germany's invasion of Russia.

Gene looks admiringly at his dad – a 33 year old tenant farmer who is six foot tall, has a full head of hair, and a welcoming smile. His father's fair-skinned face is weathered and tanned from working outdoors. The straw hat he wears all summer protects his forehead from the sun, but it does little to protect his face, creating what is known as a farmer's tan – a white forehead with a russet-colored face.

Gene walks like his father, looks like his father, and attempts to talk like him. He is energetic asking questions of people, looking for critters when playing outdoors, and often visiting imaginary places. The summer sun has lightened Gene's reddish brown hair and formed freckles on his face. In the winter the freckles dissolve, and he is left with his father's skin. The boy especially enjoys running free in the wooded areas on the farm, except on Saturday nights when he and his father attend a movie in Jefferson.

"That Gene Autry sure can sing," praises the five-year old as he admires the singing cowboy. Only cowboy and low budget detective movies are shown at the Howard Theater. If you want to enjoy the Oscar possibilities, you'll need to pay extra at the Iowa Theater at the other end of town. Cowboy movies like *Dodge City, Mexicali Rose,* and *Days of Jesse James* are enjoyed at the Howard by preteens and their fathers. Western movies like *Stagecoach* with John Wayne or *Destry Rides Again* starring Jimmy Stewart are shown at the Iowa Theater and aren't really cowboy movies according to the young boy. He believes that neither Wayne nor Stewart are real cowboys because they do not have a special horse nor do they sing.

"You like Gene Autry because he has the same name as you," teases his dad.

"Nope," replies Gene. "Gene Autry can ride better and has a faster horse than other cowboys."

"If Roy Rogers was called Gene, then you'd like Rogers more."

"No," Gene shouts, raising his voice as they walk toward Shuey's Drug store.

After the movie, it's a Saturday night ritual that they stop at the drug store. Gene is given two pennies to buy some penny candy, and his dad occasionally buys a tin of Prince Albert tobacco for making hand-rolled cigarettes.

While Gene deliberates between buying a roll of cellophane wrapped mints called Smarties Candy Rolls or a small pack of candy cigarettes, his dad waits for him outside the store. Through the window Gene studies his dad hand rolling a cigarette. He fills the cigarette paper with loose tobacco then licks the thin paper that seals the tobacco inside. His dad places the crude cigarette between his lips, strikes a farmer's match on a lamp post to light it, and inhales the smoke. That makes Gene's choice easier, and he buys the candy cigarettes. Gene pays the clerk two cents for the candy and leaves the store. Gene now inhales the evening air and pretends to exhale smoke as the two continue their discussion about cowboys.

"Tom Mix, now there's a cowboy," taunts his dad.

"Mix is a good cowboy Dad, but he's old," says Gene challenging his dad's favorite.

Tom Mix, from the silent movie era, has lost his popularity to Hopalong Cassidy, Roy Rogers, and Gene Autry. These recent actors have become heroes to young boys, and they promote codes for respectable behavior. Gene's Uncle Frank gave him a copy of the Cowboy Code created by Gene Autry.

1. A cowboy must never shoot first, hit a small man, or take unfair advantage.
2. A cowboy must never go back on his word.
3. A cowboy must always tell the truth.
4. A cowboy must be gentle to small children, old folks, and animals.
5. A cowboy must be free from racial and religious intolerances.
6. A cowboy must help people in distress.
7. A cowboy must be a good worker.
8. A cowboy must respect women, parents, and his nation's laws.
9. A cowboy must keep himself clean in thought, speech, action, and personal habits.
10. A cowboy must be a patriot.

His father had read the ten principles to Gene and explained that they are good beliefs to follow. While Gene doesn't understand the principles completely, he understands that fighting is a poor way to solve problems.

Thinking of the newsreel about Germany's invasion of Russia, Gene asks, "Why are the two countries fighting?"

"Germany is pretty much at war with everyone," replies his dad.

"Will we go to war?"

"No," his Dad's answers quickly, almost too quickly, but convincingly enough to satisfy the five year old.

The boy and his father continue their walk in silence, enjoying the peaceful evening as Gene sucks sugar from his candy and his dad continues to draw in nicotine from the self-made cigarette. They join Gene's two brothers and his mother, who have purchased the weekly groceries and are visiting with neighbors about the past week's events and upcoming activities. The family climbs into a four-door 1933 Chevy and heads north to their farm located a mile north and three miles west of Jefferson.

Gravel roads lead to the eighty-acre Ulrich Farm where Gene lives with his family. In the spring the ditches are full of wild strawberries, plum bushes, and poison ivy. In the fall the ditches reveal milkweeds and cattails especially near the low lying marshy areas.

The long lane leading from the gravel road to the house is as full of surprises as the Yellow Brick Road in the *Wizard of Oz*. Wild roses climb over foxtails and sandburs growing in the ditches along the narrow lane, and in the spring the hilly pasture is a carpet of dandelions hiding beneath wild daisies. Honey bees buzz around the dandelions, and collect nectar from the yellow flowers. The farm scenery changes every season and brings surprises in the springtime with the birth of new calves, piglets, and kittens born in the barn's hayloft.

In the summer the huge burr oaks hide the summer sun and provide nests for the squirrels. When fall arrives, acorns drop from the trees providing food for the squirrels, and Gene rakes the leaves into large piles where he hides and lies quietly. He feels secure and protected under the large mound of oak leaves while the squirrels and an occasional rabbit discover him spying on their world. In the winter the narrow dirt lane becomes packed with snow and provides a slope where Gene slides on a shovel that is used to scoop snow in the winter and corn in the fall.

The lane leading to the house is no Yellow Brick Road for his parents. In the winter it is blocked with snow and in the spring impassable because the spring rains turn it into a muddy quagmire. His dad is forced to leave their 1933 Chevrolet parked at the end of the lane. The car remains there until the family uses it to go shopping on Saturday and church on Sunday. What's more, in the summer you wouldn't find a scarecrow, lion, or tin man skipping along with Dorothy. Instead, the dry wind blows the dust from the dirt lane into the house. No, this isn't the Land of OZ. It's rural Iowa in 1941.

The house and the farm buildings lie between forty tillable acres to the north, and a hilly pasture to the south full of giant burr oaks and gnarly cedar trees. Twisting around at the base of the hills is a small meandering stream, which leads to the Raccoon River. The only useful purpose for the tree-covered pasture is to provide a grazing area for the farm animals. More importantly to Gene is that it provides a playground for him and his two older brothers.

The winding stream is a private place for Gene and his brothers to play. They build mud dams in the creek, and on hot summer afternoons they cool off in the trapped muddy water. After a downpour the rock and stick barriers wash away, giving the boys an opportunity to improve their engineering skills.

The house is a two-story farmhouse that needs painting. Its worn shingles and weathered wood siding are in part protected by three large burr oaks. Additional oaks merge with cedar scrubs down the hill until willows take control at the bottom of the hill. In the winter the house is drafty, and Gene's dad nails tarpaper around the lower outside of the home to keep the winter wind from invading. There is no modern plumbing and no electricity. Drinking water is pumped from a hand pump located about forty yards west of the house. A rain barrel catches water from a downspout that is used for washing clothes.

There are no modern conveniences, and the outhouse is fifty yards east of the house. Family members waste no time when using the privy and doing their business. In the winter it becomes an especially quick trip when the temperatures fall below freezing. A chamber pot is placed on the enclosed porch and is available for those needing to go to the toilet on cold winter nights. The next morning it is dumped in the outdoor privy, and washed and scrubbed by the person who used it during the night. In the summer a sticky fly strip is fastened to the ceiling of the outdoor toilet to reduce the number of flies.

The Des Moines Register and a battery-operated radio are the daily connections to the world. Saturday's movie newsreels provide a visual capsule of the weekly world events. At night the family listens to radio programs like the *Lone Ranger* and *Mystery Theater*. During the day Gene's mom listens to *Kitchen Clatter* from Shenandoah, Iowa, and her two favorite soap operas *One Man's Family* and *Lorenzo Jones and His Wife Bell*.

There are few farm buildings: a barn in need of repair, a chicken shed, the traditional Iowa corncrib, and a hog house that Gene's dad built. The rental agreement between the landlord, Mrs. Theresa Ulrich, and Gene's parents provides her with half of the cash from the sale of grain produced on the farm. The contract permits his parents the use of the pasture and the farm buildings where they raise about fifty chickens, four cows, two work horses, and two sows. The sows give birth to a total of twelve to sixteen piglets each year. Mrs. Ulrich lives in Jefferson and does little to maintain the buildings. The Great Depression of the 1930s is still being felt in rural Iowa, and there aren't resources to apply toward the upkeep of farm buildings.

Returning from the weekly Sunday mass, Gene carefully removes his "Sunday Clothes." He drapes his dress pants over a wooden hanger and places them in the closet, kicks off his black shoes, which are a size too large and hand-me-downs from his older brother, and places them in the closet, and throws his shirt on the bed for his mom to collect for Monday's wash. He then changes into his familiar frayed overalls and hurries downstairs. It's a hot August afternoon, so he wears neither a shirt nor shoes. In the dining/living room he joins his mom, dad and two brothers for Sunday dinner consisting of fried chicken, milk gravy, new potatoes, green beans, and tomatoes harvested from the large family garden. There is fresh lemonade to drink.

After excusing himself from the dinner table, Gene disappears into the tree and scrub covered pasture south of the house. He pretends to be a cowboy as he rides his imaginary pony searching for snakes, frogs, and crawdads that can be found on the banks of the meandering creek hid by the willow trees.

He hides under some low willow branches that sweep the surface of the stream and hopes to catch a glimpse of a thirsty deer. But soon he is startled when a young rabbit invades his hiding place and hops quickly up the slope toward the house.

During the summer Gene's reddish-brown uncombed hair is lightened several shades by the sun and answers only to wind. And after an afternoon of playing, it is difficult to tell where the dirt ends and suntan begins on his neck since they are equally dispersed. A scrubbing of soap and water usually cleans him sufficiently before supper and bed, but this evening a full bath is needed.

A round galvanized tub hangs in the shanty attached to the kitchen and is used for Saturday baths. Gene took the traditional Saturday night bath, but he is taking another one this evening. This is a tad unusual, but tomorrow is going to be a special day. Gene's mother removes the galvanized bath tub from the shanty. She places the tub between the kitchen table and a cream-colored enamel wood-burning range. His mother pats her brow with her red gingham apron; heating water on the range in late August makes the small kitchen as hot as a Lakota sweat lodge. She pours water into the tub and checks the water's temperature with her index finger.

Satisfied with the temperature, she calls, "Gene, it's time for your bath."

Gene runs into the kitchen wearing only his shorts and heads for the tub filled with warm water. He looks at his mother before removing his shorts and declares, "I'm taking my bath now."

"I know."

"Well, you can leave; I am old enough to wash myself."

"Okay," she replies, as she smiles to herself. "I promise not to watch, but I will wash the supper dishes while you bathe."

Gene slips off his shorts and steps into the tub. He starts scrubbing his slender body and splashes water on the weathered pine floor as he concentrates on getting clean. He's oblivious to his mother and his surroundings as he scrubs his knees and elbows covered with a combination of fresh dirt, scrapes, and scabs. Gene stops scrubbing long enough to look at his mother who is resting in a chair waiting for him to finish.

A strand of her red curly hair dangles slightly over her forehead and her fair complexion highlights the sprinkling of freckles around her nose. Gene enjoys his mom and learns from her bizarre sense of humor, like the time she covered small pieces of soap with chocolate and told him not eat any while she went outside to feed the chickens. He disobeys and eats one of the forbidden candies. Instantly he begins foaming at the mouth, and learns to follow her directions. He learns from her practical jokes, and prefers to be taught lessons from her pranks more than her quick backhand that is sometimes used to enforce her rules.

Tonight he is making sure there is no dirt left on his body. One of her rules is to be well groomed when leaving the farm meaning dirt free, clean clothes, hair combed and teeth brushed. She often reminds him that even if they have little money there is no excuse for being dirty or wearing dirty clothes in public. Soap is cheap.

She seems especially happy tonight and Gene willingly completes his bath, dries himself with a faded blue towel, and puts on a clean pair of shorts. After telling his mom and dad goodnight and promising to say his prayers, Gene climbs the narrow staircase to his bedroom. Morning will come soon.

The morning sun brightens the small bedroom even with the shade drawn to keep the sun from invading the room, and the sound of mourning doves awakens the young boy. There is a bed pressed against the north wall that is shared by Gene's two brothers. Gene's smaller bed hugs the south wall and separating the beds is a dresser that holds all of their underclothes, socks and shirts.

His older brothers have left the room and are finishing their chores. Fearing he is late, Gene leaps out of bed, slips into his faded jeans and scuffed shoes. He then hurries to the hen house to gather eggs, a chore he is expected to do every morning. This morning he wants to finish quickly so he gathers only eggs in the nests without hens, knowing that the hens sitting on nests will peck at his hand if he bothers them. The missed eggs will be collected tonight.

Returning to the kitchen, he sets the basket of eggs down and washes his hands and face in the porcelain basin that is on the washstand. He helps himself to warm oatmeal that his mother has prepared and left on the kitchen stove and gulps down a glass of fresh milk.

Gene hustles upstairs and struggles into his stiff, new Oshkosh bib overalls, and squeezes his feet into the new brown leather shoes that have never been worn. The new overalls aren't as comfortable as the frayed ones he wore the last few months, but they have pockets where he can stash unusual rocks and even conceal a milkweed pod. He especially likes the pocket on the bib where he can hide special treasures, which can be snapped shut with a metal snap. As for shoes, he seldom wore any in the summer except when going to town or to keep his feet clean after bathing. Shoes of any kind feel awkward. He even brushes his hair because it is September 1, 1941, and he wants to look good for his first day of school.

He scurries down the stairs, out the door, and jumps into the front seat of the 1933 Chevrolet. He carries his new olive-colored oval lunch bucket, which contains a sandwich wrapped in wax paper to keep it fresh. It's a bologna sandwich made with store-bought bread and lots of homemade butter. Also packed in the lunch pail are two freshly baked peanut butter cookies and a Jonathon apple picked from the tree in the backyard.

Gene clutches a Big Chief writing tablet with an American Indian in a full headdress on the cover, and Gene assumes that all Indians look like the Lakota Chief. He also carries a pencil box given to him by his Aunt Nell. Inside the box are eight crayons: black, brown, orange, violet, blue, green, red, and yellow that fit tightly in the new Crayola box. Eight colors are enough if he doesn't lose them, break them, or if a neighbor boy named Henry doesn't eat them. His brothers have warned Gene that Henry, who also attends Bristol 7, sometimes eats glue and crayons.

Gene once overheard his mom tell his dad, "Something needs to be done about Henry. He rules the Henderson household and doesn't know the meaning of discipline."

Additional supplies protected in the pencil box include two pencils, a pair of round tipped scissors, and a six inch ruler. His Aunt Nell has added two pink erasers since she has observed Gene's need to erase, and when he rubs too hard he leaves holes in the paper. Aunt Nell is his mom's older sister who lives in Jefferson, Iowa, and on special occasions invites Gene to sleep overnight with her and his Uncle Frank. At their home he bathes in a tub, which is filled with water from a faucet, sleeps alone in a featherbed, and uses the magnificent white porcelain wash basin, which is filled with hot water directly from a faucet. These comforts aren't found in his farm home, so when staying overnight in their home he feels as if he is a guest in one of the fancy homes seen in the movies.

Beneath the box of school supplies is the *Come and Play* pre-reading workbook. It features Tom and Nancy, as well as Tom's dog Sandy, and Nancy's dog Shep. Gene looks at the pictures and wonders if where they live there are oak trees, a muddy stream, and marshy areas where milkweeds grow.

His mom opens the car door, interrupting his daydreaming and gives him her legendary hygiene inspection. A quick and not-so-gentle check confirms that he has brushed his teeth and washed behind his ears. She flattens the rooster tail, which pops up in the back of his head like a cobra ready to strike. Relieved that he has passed the inspection, Gene returns to his day dreaming only to be ordered out of the car.

"Stand over there in front of the barn," directs his mom. "I need a picture of your first day of school."

It is a two mile ride to the one-room rural school where Gene will start kindergarten, which is called the primary grade. The straight Iowa gravel roads divide the landscape into a green patchwork in the spring, and in autumn the countryside becomes a checkered mix of crisp brown cornstalks and bronzed pastures. The shallow ditches are a collage of Canada wild rye, foxtail, poison ivy, wild plum bushes, and isolated mulberry trees. The grasses, weeds, and scrubs are changing to red, orange, and various shades of brown creating a multicolored border along the road. Hiding beneath the undergrowth are pheasant nests needing repair and field mice hiding kernels of corn for winter snacks. From the car window Gene focuses on the milkweeds that are preparing to explode. He feels the milkweed pod he hid in his bib overall pocket. He likes milkweed pods and enjoys the incredible story his dad has told him about the Monarch butterflies.

Gene discovered one of the colorful cocoons, and his dad explained that Monarchs arrive in Iowa each spring and that the mother butterflies lay eggs that become caterpillars. The caterpillars spin cocoons, which turn into butterflies. This life cycle continues for four generations from Mexico until their return to Mexico. The fourth generations of Monarchs are emerging from their cocoons now as Gene begins school. Some of these special butterflies have already begun their journey south, and milkweeds are the sole source of food for their entire life. That is why his dad cautioned Gene, "Don't pick the chrysalises or disturb the yellow, white, and black striped caterpillars that feed on the milkweed leaves."

From the car window, Gene sees that some pods have exploded allowing the wind to carry the seeds to new areas where they will take root, grow into new plants, and provide food for next spring's Monarchs. His dad told him that the milkweeds have been in Iowa for years and that the Native Americans made twine from the coarse fibers of the milkweed stalk and boiled the tender buds to eat in the spring. He said that even sugar can be extracted from the blossoms in the early spring.

Now the milkweeds are seen as a nuisance to farmers, but the story instills a curiosity in Gene and a desire to learn more about the outdoors. He enjoys chasing the fluffy clumps of silk when the pods burst and playing with the green spindle shaped pods that are about the size of duck eggs and covered with small, wiggly, wormlike soft spikes. A single pod is the right size to hide in the front pocket on his new overalls. He smiles knowing that the milkweed pod he carries has not burst – yet.

The car stops abruptly in front of the freshly painted white one-room country school. The memories of his dad's outdoor lecture on milkweeds is cut short as he focuses on the school sign centered above the two front doors – Bristol 7.

The school was built in 1874 and has one entrance that was used for boys and the other for girls twenty years earlier. Fortunately, the 1930s progressive education recommendations removed the segregation of sexes and by 1941 boys and girls entered the same door and are seated according to age or grade and not sex. Not all aspects of the school are integrated since two out-houses hide behind the school, one for boys and one for girls.

Gene steps out of the car and shifts his weight from one foot to another while his two older brothers take their school supplies inside. They then run off to join friends playing on the rusty merry-go-round beneath a large elm tree. His mom motions for him to follow her as she enters the door leading into a cloak room. They are met by a small, stout woman in her late thirties wearing a calico print cotton dress decorated with small flowers. Her black hair is pulled back and combed into a bun.

"Good morning, Miss Frohling. This is Gene," introduces his mother.

"We're so pleased to have you join us Gene," responds Miss Frohling with a large smile. She then turns to Gene's mother and replies, "You can pick him up at noon, as you know first year primary students only attend school for half a day."

His mother replies, "That's why I'm here. It's a two mile drive to school, and I don't want Gene to walk home by himself. Is it possible for him to stay for the full day and then walk home with his bothers?

As you see I'm going to be busy in the next couple of months, and it will help me greatly if Gene can stay here all day."

Miss Frohling observing that Gene's mother is expecting makes a swift appraisal of the situation and asks Gene, "If you stay all day do you promise not to interrupt the other students and to take a nap in the afternoon?"

Gene glances at his mom, peeks at the teacher, and instantly nods his head yes.

"He'll be obedient, and if he isn't let me know," is the quick response from Gene's mother. Another rule for her children is to obey teachers.

"We'll give it a try," confirms Miss Frohling. "But should Gene become disruptive, he will be restricted to one-half day of school."

"Don't worry. He won't cause you any problems. If he leaves his seat without permission, sasses, or bothers another student I want to know immediately," replies Gene's mother as she begins to leave the school. She drives away on the dusty road, leaving Gene in the cloakroom with Miss Frohling. His mother is relieved that Gene and his two older brothers are in school. She will now have two months to prepare for the arrival of her fourth child.

Looking around the cloakroom, Gene sees wooden pegs for hanging coats and caps and a space beneath the pegs for storing boots on rainy and snowy days. Across from the coat hooks is a wooden bench for sitting to remove stubborn boots or to retie a tangled shoelace. Next to the bench is a cabinet holding a stoneware crock water jar. A shelf holds several metal cups and one black and white enamel dipper. The cups belong to students who have brought them for their individual use while the community dipper is shared by students who failed to bring a cup and for those in a hurry to quench their thirst.

"You can place your lunch bucket on the shelf with the other lunches," directs Mrs. Frohling.

He adds his lunch bucket to a collection of lard tins, metal syrup pails, and a scattering of oval-shaped buckets all containing lunches. He is ushered into the one-room classroom and immediately sees a large cast iron potbelly stove with a stove pipe that stretches to the opposite side of the room. There are three windows on the east side of the room, allowing the morning light to brighten the classroom. On the west wall there are also three windows that allow the afternoon sun to create shadows on desks. There are no windows on the north wall that is covered with a large slate blackboard. Students work arithmetic problems and play tick-tack-toe on the board. The next day assignments are also written on the board for students to copy before leaving school. An alphabet is displayed directly above the blackboard in both the upper and lower case, and above the alphabet are portraits of George Washington and Abraham Lincoln.

Miss Frohling asks Gene to take a seat in the front row directly in front of a large globe atop a pedestal. Another student is already seated in the desk next to Gene.

"This is Henry, and he is in first grade," The boys take a glance at each other, neither responds. Gene, remembering the advice given by his brothers tightens the grip on his pencil box and looks carefully at Henry who is overweight, has small eyes that are close together, and a flat nose. His black hair is tangled like dog fur, but cleaner. He is wearing tattered and faded overalls and pinned on the bib of his overalls is a shiny Hopalong Cassidy badge.

Gene's first month of school is uneventful except when Henry fibs to the teacher that Gene is eating glue. The teacher does nothing since Henry is infamous for lying. Gene encounters some difficulty when learning the alphabet. He can go from A B C to R S T without coaching. But he stumbles over the last six letters. Is it U V W X Y Z or W V U X Y Z? The teacher doesn't seem worried and believes Gene will eventually learn the correct order for U and W.

In October Gene's baby brother arrives and the only change is that his new brother replaces him as the baby of the family, a status he is willing to surrender since he doesn't like being called the baby. Gene is more interested in cowboy movies and newsreels than he is in his new brother. The baby rarely cries, sleeps a lot, and is rather boring when he's awake; at least the newsreels are exciting, showing Japanese hostilities in China or showing pictures of the British fighting Nazi Germany.

After attending the movies, Gene often asks his mother questions about the war scenes. "You worry too much," too much is her normal response, but the newsreels increase his interest in foreign countries, and he creates a game with the school's globe.

He spins it, stops it with his finger, and asks Miss Frohling, "What's the name of this country?" The game annoys her, and whenever he starts the maddening inquisition she assigns extra activity work in his pre-reader. If he hesitates, she threatens him with a nap on the World War I cot hidden in the rear of the room.

Sunday, December 7, 1941, creates an urgency to learn more about the newsreel countries, and on the following Monday Gene dashes to the basketball-sized globe, spins it, and yells, "Does anyone know where Japan is?" The globe game becomes more than a game. "Where is Japan?" he asks raising his voice as he gives the globe a spin. "It is all my parents talk about."

"Slow down," Miss Frohling answers. She seems more interested in assigning poems for students to memorize for the upcoming Christmas program than in world events.

As more students enter the school, they gather around the globe and all look for Japan. Alice, an eighth grade student, joins the group. She points to the Pacific Ocean, the Hawaiian Islands, and then singles out Japan. "There's Japan, that little island off the coast of China." The students bombard Alice with questions.

"How far away is it?"

"Why did they bomb us?"

"What is war?"

Gene asks, "Will we get bombed?"

"Don't worry," Alice assures him. "We are far from the bombing that happened at Pearl Harbor."

Miss Frohling rings the bell for school to begin.

Gene moves to his desk and salutes the flag as is done every morning using the Bellamy salute, right arm extended with the palm downward and ending the pledge with the palm upwards. The extended arm is similar to the salute used in Germany, but the pledge is American and has been memorized by Gene, "I pledge Allegiance to the Flag of the United States of America and to the Republic for which it stands, one nation, indivisible, with liberty and justice for all."

After the pledge Gene's assignment is to cut out and color a picture of a Christmas tree that Miss Frohling will place in a window. The neatest and best colored trees are placed in the center windows, and those that are colored poorly or have jagged edges are buried in the bottom row of windows. Gene's art is always placed on the bottom row.

The teacher delights in keeping the windows covered with student-colored pictures. She kills two birds with one stone: her art assignments keep the students busy and she has monthly window decorations. In September it was oak leaves cut out of construction paper. In October it was Jack-O-Lanterns and in November turkeys with brown, orange, and yellow tail feathers. The windows are a virtual yearly calendar for anyone driving by the school. Now in December the windows will be adorned with brightly decorated Christmas trees.

Gene's attention drifts between thinking about Pearl Harbor and dreaming about the Christmas toys in the Montgomery Ward Catalog.

"Stop your day dreaming, Gene, and color the Christmas tree," directs Miss Frohling.

He knows if he fails to color the tree, or is too slow, she will inform his mother and he will be unable to stay in school for the full day. His mother will be required to pick him up at noon, and she will be unhappy. Gene likes school, but he wants to learn more and misses the freedom of climbing trees and helping around the house.

Last winter he helped his mother make rag rugs. She sewed the strips of old sheets, shirts, and dresses together and he sat by the sewing machine and rolled the strips into balls. She then took the balls to

Mrs. Ford, who owned a rug loom, and wove the material into area rugs. After the rugs were completed, he examined the patterns to see if he could find fabric from an old shirt or worn-out dress. His younger brother will probably take that job away from him now.

Miss Frohling glares at Gene, "Have you started coloring your tree?"

Gene likes to surprise people with the colors he chooses. For instance, cows are sometimes red and pigs are blue, and this tree will probably end up any color but green. He slowly takes the pencil box out from his desk and looks for the orange crayon.

"Where's my orange?" asks Gene.

Henry sniggers and whispers, "Did you eat it?"

"Not my orange for lunch – I don't eat crayons, I think you took it."

"Finders Keepers," Henry replies.

"Not if it's my color. You stole it," Gene answers quickly, turns, and frowns at Henry.

Miss Frohling, sensing a fight to begin, demands, "What's going on?"

"He stole my crayon. Last week he took my red color and put it in his pencil box."

"How did I know it was yours?" Henry snapped.

"Gene, come with me." Miss Frohling grabs his arm and leads him to the back of the room. She sits him on the army cot. "Are you causing problems? Last week it was the explosion of the milk-weed pod releasing hundreds of little white seeds floating around the room. I told you to take the pod home and you forgot. Now you're fighting with Henry. You're always playing with that globe. If you can't start behaving properly, I'll tell your mother."

Miss Frohling didn't want to report him to his mother, nor did she want the wrath of his mother's Irish temper. She just wants Gene to follow instructions. She can tolerate his crazy coloring; a blue pumpkin or a speckled red and green turkey like he did last month, but she insists he does what she asks and to cut carefully.

She told his mother, "Cutting is too important in developing coordination to leave it to chance." Actually she is thinking of her window decorations. She believes her art work reflects her teaching, so the drawing each mouth needs to look neat and not as if a dog has been chewing on it. Gene hates the cutting assignments as much as his teacher delights in her window decorations. It is difficult cutting with the small round-tip scissors, and he struggles with the exercise. He barely achieves her expectations while biting his lower lip and squinting at the drawings. The first month he developed blisters on his thumb, but now the blisters have become calluses and the cutting isn't as painful – just frustrating.

"I'll behave, just make Henry give me my orange color," pleads Gene.

"OK, but you must concentrate more Gene and don't let Henry trouble you," answers Miss Frohling. Henry gives the color to Miss Frohling, and Gene completes coloring the tree a dark orange and then struggles to cut it out.

After lunch Miss Frohling directs the students to place their books inside their desks. The regular schedule is altered, and everyone shifts to a more interesting task – preparing for the Christmas program. Gene looks forward to his first rural school Christmas program and his baptism at a theatrical performance.

"We are now going to prepare for the Christmas program," she tells the students as she assumes the role of drama coach.

"First, we must make a temporary stage where we can perform."

Miss Frohling directs the older students to string a wire from one side of the classroom to the other. Then she instructs them to attach bed sheets to the wire with safety pins, allowing the sheets to be closed or opened. In less than an hour the classroom is transformed into a makeshift stage worthy of a Shakespearian drama, or at least a Bristol 7 Christmas program.

Auditions aren't held. Tryouts aren't needed since Miss Frohling has predetermined the cast. Alice, the petty eighth grade girl, is cast as Mary in the reenactment of the birth of Christ. Mary is the most coveted role in the entire program, no acting needed – just sit, smile, and listen to everyone sing, "Silent Night." Gene's oldest brother will be Joseph; his other brother plus two fifth grade boys will be wise men. Gene and Henry are cast as shepherds. Most students are handed a poem and told to memorize the poem since they will recite it at the Christmas program, which is only two weeks away.

The students practice every afternoon until the day of the performance. There is no electricity in the school, and the Iowa winter sun is casting long shadows by late afternoon. The program will be held from one until three on the afternoon before Christmas vacation begins.

Parents and community members gather in the small classroom to enjoy the annual program. The bombing of Pearl Harbor is still on the minds of the adults, but Gene is focused on the most exciting school event he has experienced so far.

A scattering of songs are sung throughout the program. The students sing "O Come All Ye Faithful," "Little Town of Bethlehem," and "Jolly Old Saint Nickolas." Alice sings "Jingle Bells" as a solo rather than recite a poem, but everyone else memorizes and recites a poem. There is a short play about Santa forgetting Christmas, which is funny, and becomes especially humorous when Henry, in his role as Santa's elf, refuses to appear on stage.

The reenactment of the Nativity is the main attraction and the closing student performance. The audience is invited to join in singing "Silent Night" at the end of the manger scene. The finale is saved for Gene's reciting a poem written by Miss Frohling titled, "That's All Folks." It features her poetry rather than Gene's public speaking ability. He is dressed as a toy soldier with both cheeks painted red and wears a tin soldier's hat made from a cylinder-shaped oatmeal box covered with red construction paper and a bill made of red construction paper.

Gene peeks from behind the curtains and then marches onto the temporary stage. He takes a deep breath and recites:

"A Merry Christmas everyone,

And at this time next year,

We hope you all will reappear.

These Christmas plays are lots of fun,

So Merry Christmas everyone."

Following the program, Santa Claus distributes an orange and a bag of brightly colored hardtack Christmas candy to the students. Santa, a woman wearing a worn red suit stuffed with pillows, looks very little like the jolly old elf, and even pre-school children know this must be Santa's helper. Students munch on Christmas cookies brought to the program by their mothers and argue about whose mom's cookies are best. The dads who stuffed themselves into the desks in the back of the room to watch the performance are now crowded into the cloak room to drink coffee and talk about the Pearl Harbor bombing. A few step outside to roll a cigarette and smoke.

Gene still dressed as the toy soldier listens to the men talk about Pearl Harbor and the attack on the Philippines and then asks, "When will the war end?"

They assure him not to worry and tell him that by next Christmas the war will be something the Japanese wish they had never started. They joke that the Japanese Empire couldn't whip an army of toy soldiers.

Alice's dad says, "They are nothing but an Empire of little people who are no match for Americans."

The men agree that the only reason they did so much damage at Pearl Harbor is because they are sneaky.

Henry's dad brags, "If the war isn't over in six months, I'll join the US Army myself and go over there and whip those SOBs."

Gene listens quietly and looks to his dad for some reassurance. His dad nods his head in agreement with the other men.

1942

"Will you be gone again tonight?" asks Gene.

"I will be. Your Aunt Nell is very ill and needs someone to be with her." replies his mom.

His aunt has been ill for several months, and since Christmas day she has been extremely ill. Gene's mom warns him of her possible death.

"Remember when Aunt Rose died, and we attended her funeral in Chicago?"

"Yes. Aunt Rose died with her baby," replies Gene. "And we stayed with Aunt Daisy when you were gone."

"Well, your Aunt Nell may also die," consoles his mother.

"Will Aunt Nell die having a baby?"

"No."

"What makes her so sick?"

"Your Aunt Nell has breast cancer, and it is a dreadful disease that doctors can't cure."

His aunt dies January 2, 1942, and when his mother tells him that her sister has died she adds, "This evening after you have taken your bath, we are going to her home to pray the rosary and say good-bye."

Gene had seen a dead person once, but he didn't know the person, and they didn't say the rosary. They went to the funeral home where people were crying near a coffin that had flowers all around it. Following the preacher's prayers, they went home.

After supper is eaten, the family leaves for Uncle Frank and Aunt Nell's large home. As they approach the home, it looks as if every light in the house is on. Light shines through the front door's stained glass window, and casts a rainbow of colors on the porch's gingerbread trim. They arrive as Father Zimmerman enters the house to lead the rosary that will be prayed in a few minutes. His aunt's coffin is positioned in front of the large parlor window. Facing the coffin is a kneeler where mourners kneel and recite a Hail Mary or the Our Father for the repose of her soul to lessen her time in purgatory.

Gene carefully approaches the coffin, steps up on the kneeler, and peaks at his aunt's body. A crucifix and rosary lie on her breast. She looks like his aunt Nell, but he doesn't know how to say good-bye. She isn't smiling, and for a brief moment he looks at her and experiences a very sad feeling like when he found the dead duckling by the creek. He then steps down, so a mourner standing behind him can kneel and say a prayer.

His mom joins some other women and a few men who are kneeling on the parlor floor. Some are wiping tears from their eyes as Father begins the rosary. "In the name of the Father, and of the Son, and of the Holy Ghost...."

Gene moves silently to the back of the room and slides into the kitchen while those in the parlor pray: "Hail Mary, full of grace the Lord is with thee, blessed art thou among women...." In the kitchen Aunt Nell's two brothers and several of her brothers-in-laws are smoking and drinking shots of Irish whiskey. Gene's dad joins them for one drink and then he disappears outside to roll and smoke a cigarette. Gene squats quietly in the corner to eavesdrop on the men as they talk politely and graciously about his aunt.

"She was a good woman, she was."

"And she worked hard."

"Not only with her own kind, but Nellie was always there to help anyone in need."

"And her laughter always brought a smile to your face."

"And strict... you didn't want to sass her."

"No...nor bring dirt into her house."

They paused for another drink. Gene rises from his sitting position and turns to enter the parlor as the rosary ends. He is met in the doorway by two women coming to the kitchen who touch his shoulder caringly. They wipe tears from their eyes, but their somber faces soon turn to smiles as they listen to the men's stories. Gene joins his mother, who is sitting on the sofa in the parlor with her rosary beads wrapped around her right hand. Gene's dad also enters the room after checking on Gene's three month old brother, who is asleep on the featherbed in the guest bedroom.

"It's time you get some sleep young man," his dad says as he places Gene's coat over his shoulders. "Your mother will be staying here with Aunt Nell's body tonight, and Aunt Leona will bring her and your younger brother home tomorrow morning."

Riding home with his older brothers, Gene asks his dad, "Why do the women say prayers, but Uncle Mart and Uncle Tom tell stories?"

"It is part of the Wake," replies his father, "and in Ireland it's the way they grieve for those who die."

"I'm going to grieve for Aunt Nell too, and I'll miss staying at her house."

He liked staying overnight at his aunt and uncle's home, escaping his cold upstairs bedroom, sleeping in the warm bed and experiencing electricity and modern plumbing.

"We'll all miss her," replies his dad.

Gene snuggles beneath a quilt made from flour sacks and worn-out clothes that protects him from the freezing temperatures. He falls asleep in the rear seat of the car as it bounces past the frozen fields of picked corn.

Several months after Nell's death, her son Francis joins the US Army. He graduated from Jefferson High School a year ago, and is leaving for boot camp. The family gathers at the train station to see him off. Gene doesn't know if his cousin was drafted or voluntarily joined. He does know that there are many men leaving the county to fight the war and that Francis is headed for boot camp to become a soldier.

As summer progresses, there is a constant stream of war news in the newspaper and in the movie newsreels. The headlines read: "Japanese Capture the Philippines," "Germans Battles in North Africa," "US Navy Defeats the Japanese at Midway," "Germans Advance into the USSR." As the war becomes more intense, Gene fears his dad will be drafted, and on a Saturday he asks, "Will you be fighting in the war?"

"I will not be going to war," answered his dad. "I'm a farmer, and farming is a critical job because our soldiers need food."

"Good ... but why did Francis go?"

"Because he wanted to join the Army," responds his dad.

"Did he have to?" asks Gene

"Yes, I think so. The government has a complex draft system, which provides guidance to the County Draft Board; they follow guidelines as to who is drafted and who isn't," Gene's dad explains. "In fact, there are twenty-one classifications and Francis was a 1A. Those classified as 1A either join or wait until the Draft Board calls them to serve."

"Oh," Gene answers not really interested in the knowing any details. He doesn't understand the draft system but has heard his mom and dad talk about it. He knows some men are drafted and some aren't.

Gene is told that healthy men are classified as a 1A and will probably be drafted into the US Army. If the men are needed at home to do critical jobs, like his dad, they are classified 2A. Men needed to care for children or parents receive a 3A classification and are even less likely to be drafted.

Those classified as a 4 are not drafted: 4A is given to those who have completed their service; men classified as 4B are deferred because they are government officials; 4C classifications identify enemy aliens; 4D are ministers; 4E are conscientious objectors or men who are too old to serve; and 4F are those judged morally, mentally, or physically unfit for service. It's the 4F label that is most misunderstood.

Last week Gene had overheard some men talking about Frederick Schmidt at Mike's Food Market in Farlin.

"Fred Schmidt is classified as 4F, that coward."

"Yeah, he's un-American, probably pro-German. His people come from Germany, you know."

"He was always afraid, even as a boy."

"Don't be hard on Fred," responds Mike, the owner of the store. "He has a bad heart; the boy's not healthy. That is why he is a 4F."

Gene repeats the story to his dad and asks, "Is Fred Schmidt a coward?"

"No," his dad responds and explains that too often when a man is classified as 4F he is labeled as a draft-dodger or a coward. Gene doesn't want his dad labeled as either, nor does he want him to be drafted. He's happy his dad is a farmer and can help the war effort at home, but there is still a fear he might need to leave home to fight the Nazis or Japanese.

His dad continues, "I am not going to be drafted and I sure as heck am not going to join the army. I have a job to help feed the troops, and I'm going to stay here and help your mother keep you out of trouble."

His dad finishes his coffee and leaves the kitchen to start the routine Saturday chores of cleaning manure from the chicken house. When finished, he checks the pasture fences for breaks where livestock might escape. Some fence posts are found that needs replacing and some barbed wire is loose. He telephones his brother Ed, to ask him for help in fixing the fence, and Ed agrees to help the following Saturday.

Saturday morning Gene's Uncle stops to help mend fences. Gene's uncle is smaller than his dad and his face reveals an injury he received from being kicked in the face by a horse. Gene has heard the story from his dad many times as a warning not to be silly-crazy and catch a horse's tail for a wild ride. When his dad was young, he and Ed would grab the tail of a horse and jump along holding onto the horse's tail. Ed got too close to the horse; the horse reared up and kicked him, catching Ed in the face. His nose was nearly torn from his face and required many stitches to be reattached.

The disfigurement didn't bother him, and he is a good-humored person who enjoys visiting with adults and children. He walks into the house and immediately asks Gene a riddle, "What gets wetter and wetter the more it dries?"

"I don't know," Gene replies.

"I'll give you a hint. You use one after a bath."

"I still don't know."

"A towel, silly. Didn't you learn anything your first year of school?"

"Maybe," Gene answers.

That isn't quite true since his grades were all above the 90th percent mark, and he received all A's and B's on his report card. His deportment was excellent, so his scraps with Henry weren't too serious, just annoying. Gene didn't learn as much as he wanted to learn. He expected to know how to read like his dad, and all he got to read was the Tom and Nancy Reading Book.

He discovers that Nancy and Tom live in a different world than he. Tom lives in a nicely painted house in the city and rides in a shiny car. Both he and Nancy travel back and forth between the city and the farm riding in trains and even ships. Nancy lives in a "never-land farm" that looks nothing like the farm he lives on. On Nancy's make-believe farm there are sheep, cows, and pigs that are always clean. The sun is always shining, pastures are full of yellow flowers, and no mud is ever brought into the house. Meanwhile the pigs on Gene's farm like to slosh around in the mud and burrow under the fences, the neighbor's sheep butt him rather than wait to be petted, and hens peck at Gene's hands when he collects eggs. It is fun reading about Nancy, but it isn't the farm Gene lives on.

He wants to learn things that his father knows and to read the newspaper and magazines. He wants to read the big-little books his older brother reads. Gene's first year isn't wasted as he can write and say the alphabet, except for the last six letters, which confuse him. He can print cow, pig, dog, and cat and is learning the names of countries that appear in the newspapers and on the movie screen. And he can find countries on the large globe that sits in front of him at school.

Arithmetic is his easiest subject. He learns quickly that numbers can be organized into groups of ten. If asked to count, Gene counts until someone begs for him to stop, something which his Uncle Ed discovered earlier.

Uncle Ed switches the subject from school and invites him to join them in fixing fences, "Someone is always needed to select the fence staples from the can and hand them to whoever is stapling the barb wire to the post."

It's true that if someone untangles the metal fasteners and hands them to the person hammering, mending the fence goes faster. Gene is excited to join his dad and uncle as they fix fences. The two men enjoy talking about the outdoors, probably because their family farmed in Greene County for years. Their grandfather was a sodbuster who broke sod in Illinois, Kansas, and the Dakotas in the 1800s before settling in Iowa. Their father farmed before he lost the homestead in the economic depression following World War I.

The two men and the boy amble along the fence row that separates the pasture from marshlands. The two older men discuss farming and the price of corn.

"You think the corn will yield fifty-five bushels an acre?"

"Yeah, and with forty acres of corn I should harvest two thousand and two hundred bushels."

"Selling it for sixty cents, maybe sixty-five cents a bushel, you'll make around one thousand and four hundred dollars."

"Yeah, but once I pay off the loans and give seven hundred dollars to the landlord I'll be lucky to clear three hundred dollars, but that is better than the two dollars and thirty-two cents that we started with in 1940. Sometimes I think I might just as well harvest those cattails. At least the Indians made good use of what was around them, and they didn't pay the landlord a cent."

The swampy marsh next to the pasture is covered with clusters of six foot cattails, and beneath them are American Coots nests. The American Coots are strange ducks that appear to be running across the water before they lift off and start flying. Sharing the marsh are the muskrats, beavers, frogs, and turtles; but it's the cattails with their cigar shaped spikes called catkins that Gene wants to learn about. Gene asks his dad, "How did the Indians use cattails?"

"They wove the stalks into mats, interlaced them to cover their wigwams, and used the fluff to insulate their boots and padding for their baby cradleboards."

"I suppose they even ate cattails?" laughs Gene.

"Yes, they did. They ground up the roots to use as flour, and the sap was used as starch in soups. They even treated blisters, infections, and stings using powder from the pounded roots."

Those were the things Gene wanted to learn from the books. He wanted to know everything his dad knew. He hopes that this fall he will start learning stuff like that rather than reading about a never-land farm.

———

In the summer of 1942, Gene's energy is committed to outdoor antics in the wooded area south of their house and building makeshift log cabins out of fallen branches and boards. He does help his mother in the garden and looks forward to seeing his cousins from Chicago when they come later in the summer.

His mom plants a large garden every spring, and as summer vacation begins there are orderly rows of lettuce, carrots, green beans, peas, and beets peeking up from beneath the black Iowa soil. She will soon be setting out tomato plants, pepper plants, and eggplants. Near the field corn, she plants potatoes and sweet corn that will be kept free of weeds by Gene's dad when he uses the horse drawn cultivator to weed the field corn.

Keeping the vegetable garden free of weeds takes work, and is everyone's responsibility. Gene's mom assigns rows of vegetables for each son to weed and hoe. If cousins from Chicago visit for a week or more, they too will be assigned some vegetables to care for. There is equity in the tasks since the older children are responsible for more rows than those who are younger. While it is equitable, the older kids sometimes complain, but not where their mother can hear. Another one of her rules: do your share without complaining. The boys know if she hears them complain they likely will be assigned an additional row.

The garden provides most of the family's food, and since his mother says, "Idle hands are the devil's workshop," all the children not only help with the weeding, but they also help in harvesting the vegetables. When the beans, peas, beets, and tomatoes are ready, Gene and his brothers assist in picking them and preparing them for the pressure cooker. Gene dislikes shelling peas the most, since the peas must be removed from the pods after they are picked and it takes a half hour for him to pod enough peas to fill a pint jar. Snipping the ends off string beans is boring, but at least he can see several dozen quarts ready for canning by the end of the morning.

Once the vegetables are removed from the pressure cooker and cooled, Gene carries the jars of fresh canned vegetables to the cool cellar where they are placed on shelves. He arranges them in orderly rows as if they are platoons of soldiers preparing for a parade. Large quart jars of string beans are positioned at the rear and the pints of peas placed in front. Room is left on the shelves for a platoon of canned corn and a squad of canned beets to complete a full company of vegetables ready to be eaten during the winter. Newly dug carrots are buried in a large porcelain crock full of sand and will be eaten during the winter months. In the far corner of the cellar is a wooden potato bin where the new potato crop will be stored.

"Will we have enough food to last all winter?" Gene asks his mom.

"We'll have plenty of food. Even during the Great Depression we never went hungry and we won't go hungry now, even if the Government begins to ration food because of the war."

"Why do we go to Jefferson and buy groceries?"

"We still need to buy salt, flour, sugar, and spices that are needed for baking and canning. We also need breakfast food, peanut butter, and a loaf of beard from the store is always a treat. "

In August, Gene's Chicago cousins arrive for ten days, and his dad sets up a large World War I army tent where his cousins and older brothers sleep. Gene is too young to sleep in the tent with the older kids and is restricted to sleeping in his upstairs bedroom. The first night he begs to join them, only to be told no, in no uncertain terms. He doesn't argue and on a hot August night, shortly before his cousins are to return to Chicago, he is happy to be sleeping inside.

Asleep in the stuffy bedroom with a light breeze blowing in the window, lightening begins illuminating the sky revealing colossal clouds that are crashing into one another. Soon the collisions create thunder that echoes across the countryside, and the sky releases buckets of rain that cool the sweltering night. Between the flashes of lightning, he watches the rainwater bounce off the tent and disappear into the darkness. Intermittently he catches a glimpse of his dad protecting the motley crew with a large blanket as he protects them from the downpour and brings them inside. The scene reminds Gene of a hen shielding her chicks under her wings, as night arrives. His brothers and cousins are crammed into the kitchen, where they are dried and put to bed on the wooden living room floor.

Following the night's thunderstorm the morning sun reveals the damage done to the landscape. The tent is collapsed, and branches litter the yard. The small meandering creek south of the house is no longer a babbling brook but is a roaring river that is out of control. By three o'clock in the afternoon the glut of water is gone, consumed by the North Raccoon, a legitimate river. There are no signs of Gene's small mud dams built in the creek, only uprooted clumps of weeds, brushwood, and sticks which cover the stream's embankment.

Gene's mom prepares the rescued campers a breakfast of scrambled eggs, fried potatoes, milk, and side pork. Today the cousins must collect their belongings, wash their clothes, and pack the suitcases so they can be ready to board the train tomorrow morning for their return to Chicago.

A week following the storm Gene and his brothers begin to prepare for school. They must purchase supplies and books, and the first stop is the Greene Country School Superintendent's Office. The superintendent, Mr. Morris, is a tall man with graying hair. He gives Gene's mother three book lists: one for the sixth grade, one for the fourth grade, and one for the first grade. Carrying the list, his mother and the three boys leave the court house, walk past the Abraham Lincoln statue that guards the Lincoln Highway, and cross the street to the south side drug store.

New text books are shelved in one section, and used textbooks are located in another section of the store. They find the used books section; the two older boys explore the fourth and sixth grade sections searching for the best used books. Gene's mother helps Gene find a first grade Tom and Nancy reader, a first grade arithmetic book, and a science book that will be used for first and second grade. They find books with few marks, and his mother reminds the boys to take good care of the books. At the end of the school year, they will sell the books back to the drug store owner. He buys only books that are in good shape, which he can resell to other students.

Gene holds tightly to the three books they have found and follows his mother to the "new book section." There they select a first grade grammar workbook. Gene holds the book to his face and breaths in the smell of printer's ink. Next, they select general school supplies. Each boy selects his own writing tablet, a jar of white paste, two new # 2 pencils, and an eraser. The older brothers select watercolor sets, bottles of ink, a dip pen, and four extra pen points called nibs. First graders are too young to use ink. Gene's oldest brother needs a fountain pen for school, but since he received one for his birthday he doesn't need to buy one.

His mother pays cash for the supplies using money from the sale of this week's eggs. Egg money is usually spent on groceries, but this week there will be fewer groceries, and more will be eaten from the garden. Educational costs are a priority, even if she or her husband needs to do with less.

School starts August 31, and the same students are returning to Bristol 7. Henry is at school when Gene arrives, and he is heavier than he was last year. He is boasting that he has better school supplies than Gene and brags about his box of forty-eight crayons. Then he crows, like a rooster swaggering in a barn yard, and reveals his new lunch bucket has a fancy thermos bottle. "I can now keep cold milk, cold, and hot chocolate, hot."

"Who needs a thermos bottle?" Gene murmurs quietly under his breath. "This school has all the water I need."

There is one significant difference when the students recite the Pledge Allegiance to the Flag. The Bellamy salute is no longer used and rather than saluting the flag with the right arm extended students now place their right hand over their heart, and they repeat the familiar words pledging allegiance to the flag and to the nation it represents.

———

In November the Greene County nurse visits the one room school to give students their vaccination shots for small pox and diphtheria. A week before the nurse's visit, a pamphlet is sent home informing the parents what to expect after the immunizations.

- Your child may have a mild fever a day after receiving the shot.
- A scab will form in a couple of days where they received the small pox shot.
- Students must keep the immunization area clean.
- Avoid scratching or touching the small pox vaccination on the shoulder.

The shots are given, and several days later Gene's smallpox area becomes red. By the end of the week a soft scab develops. The spot vacillates between hurting and itching, but Gene doesn't scratch the area and washes his hands as directed. In three weeks the dry scab falls off by itself, leaving a red scar on his upper arm.

Henry isn't as careful and infects himself by scratching the immunization and transfers the vaccinia to his elbow, creating a second scab. He then runs a fever and misses school for nearly a month. When he returns to school he shows everyone his pox marks, one on his shoulder and one on his elbow. Students make fun of Henry, saying he can't keep his hands to himself. In reality he didn't follow instructions and transferred the small pox vaccine to another part of his body, creating a second small pox.

After checking the student's immunizations the county nurse recommends that the students stop using the water bucket with the common dipper, and suggests that the school purchase a new automatic water dispenser. The school director buys a new water crock with a simple spout that releases water when the student pushes a metal button, and requires all students to bring individual drinking cups, as there will be no more "community dipper." Even though Henry brings his cup, none of the students want their cup placed near his.

"He may still have small pox."

"If he can't keep his hands to himself, he may grab my cup."

The more the kids pick on Henry, the more Gene feels sorry for him; however, Gene isn't about to place his cup next to Henry's and looks for ways to avoid him. Gene even asks Miss Frohling if he can help her, so he won't have to be next to Henry. She is pleased to keep the two apart and sometimes asks Gene to make copies of pictures using the mimeograph pan.

The mimeograph pan is full of a jelly-like substance that is kept on a shelf behind the teacher's desk. To make multiple copies, she draws or writes on a mimeograph master sheet and then presses the master sheet on the pan of jelly. When she removes the mimeograph master, a reverse imprint of whatever is on the master mimeograph sheet is left on the jelly's surface. Gene carefully presses a clean sheet of regular paper on the pan of jelly and then he lifts the paper just as cautiously. Bravo! One by one he makes duplicate copies. By the miracle of science, the drawing is transferred from the pan of jelly to the clean sheet of paper.

When a new imprint is needed, the jelly is wiped clean using a solvent. However, after several uses of the jelly, the cleaning solvent and past pictures are mixed so the pan is warmed on the potbelly stove where the jelly slowly melts. At the end of the day, it is removed to cool. By the following morning, all traces of the past drawing are gone, and the jelly is ready to use again. Helping his teacher makes Gene feel important, and it is better than being pestered by Henry.

Miss Frohling realizes that Gene needs more work to keep him from getting into trouble, so she loans him a copy of the Elson Basic Reader from her library. It is filled with children's poems, stories about pet rabbits, and visits to farms. The characters in the book live in homes much like those in the Tom and Nancy reading books, but not like his home.

Gene memorizes a poem about a see-saw and if anyone asks if he is learning anything in school, he recites the poem.

"Polly has a pony,
A pony white and brown
And Billy has a wagon
To take him into town.
But I have made a see-saw,
And it goes up and down."

Still he doesn't escape the dreaded art classes, and he returns to coloring and cutting out drawing for the windows. This year they are more difficult. In October it is a witch for Halloween, a pilgrim for November, and snowflakes for December.

A traditional one room school Christmas program is held on the afternoon that school is dismissed for the 1942 Holiday vacation. Gene is a shepherd for the nativity scene, and *God Bless America* is added as the last song to be sung. After the program there is little discussion about the war since the men are concerned about a winter storm that is developing. However, the war that was dismissed last Christmas as a small conflict is now raging across Europe, Africa and the Pacific. There is no candy distributed this year, but Santa Claus hands out apples and popcorn balls. Because of the approaching snow storm, the families round up their children once Santa makes his appearance and head for home.

The rationing of sugar and coffee started five months into the war, and by the end of 1942 there is rationing of many items including canned food and meat. The government is concerned about the shortage of items, but they are also troubled by people hoarding supplies. Gene is concerned about the rationing of toys, and while toys aren't rationed there is a shortage of metal and rubber, making toys difficult to obtain.

"There won't be many toys this year," Gene's mother informs the family. "But we will be okay. We can always cut down a Christmas tree by the creek, bring it home, and decorate it."

"Let's go looking for the best Christmas tree in Greene County," Gene challenges his dad.

His dad answers, "I'll grab the ax, and we'll drive over by Conroy's farm and walk along the hills. We should discover the perfect tree."

They trod though the knee-high snow looking for a tree that might model for a Currier and Ives Christmas card. Discovering none that are symmetrical or with full braches, they settle for a squatty red cedar. His dad chops down the four foot tree, and they both pull it through the snow to the car. They slide it into the back seat and return home. Arriving home, Gene runs ahead. "Mom we got a great tree, not too tall, not too short, and not too many branches." His dad begins trimming the tree on the front porch and prepares to set it in a bucket of sand.

"It's a shrub cedar," Gene's mother explodes when she sees the destitute tree. "Is there a shortage of trees, too?"

"There are no Blue Spruce or Scotch Pine trees growing along the Hardin Creek. Only cedar shrubs, and with no money to buy a tree this will have to do," his dad answers.

"I'm tired of doing without. During the Depression there was no money and now because of the war everything is rationed or not available." She storms into the house.

"Going without is getting old, and we may be fighting this war for a long time, but we'll be fine," Gene's dad replies as the door slams.

Feeling disappointed Gene adds "I wish this war was over. Why do countries fight?"

His mother is cooled down when Gene and his dad bring the tree inside. She has a box of glass ornaments in the shapes of pine cones, balls, and acorns and some tinsel, called icicles, to decorate the tree. She and Gene begin hanging the decorations and tinsel on the sparsely branched tree. His mother reminds Gene again, "Santa is working hard to fight this war, so there won't be much for Christmas this year."

On Christmas Eve 1942, Gene's Uncle Frank calls from Jefferson and announces that Santa has left Jefferson and is heading north. Gene runs upstairs because he knows that if Santa catches him awake there may be no toys at all. His older brothers beat Gene to the bedroom and block him from looking down the heat register that allows heat from the first floor to flow upstairs.

"Ho, Ho, Ho," Gene hears Santa laugh, and he crowds closer to the register.

"Get back; you don't want Santa to see you," his brothers whisper.

When the kitchen door slams shut, Gene's mother announces that Santa has left and for them to come down stairs to see the gifts. Hurrying down stairs, Gene finds his sock filled with hard Christmas candy and an orange. Beside his sock are fifteen toy cardboard soldiers; two riding motorcycles, eight running with rifles, three lying on their stomachs aiming a rifle, and Gene's favorite; a soldier behind a machine gun. The models are held upright by cardboard stands and Gene starts setting them up. His mom explains there will be time to play with the soldiers tomorrow after Mass, but for now he is to climb back upstairs and get into bed.

1943

"They're all dead," Gene's mom informs his dad as he enters the kitchen after doing his morning chores.

"Who is dead?" he asks.

"The Sullivan brothers, it's on the morning news," she replies and adds a shovel full of corncobs to the kitchen range. She replaces the round black lid on the range and thinks about her own four sons. She then whispers to herself, "That poor mother, all of her five boys died at the same time and on the same ship."

Over the next six months the Sullivan brothers' deaths are reported fully in the newspapers and on the radio. The five were serving aboard the USS Juneau when it was torpedoed by a Japanese submarine, killing all five brothers. It occurred at the battle of Guadalcanal in November 1942, but the full story is being released now. The two oldest brothers had served in the United States Navy and had been honorably discharged. They reenlisted. And when their three younger brothers joined the Navy, it was with the understanding that the five would not be separated. The tragedy results in the enforcement of the existing policy of not assigning siblings to the same unit or ship.

President Roosevelt and Pope Pius XII send letters expressing their grief for the family's loss, and the heartbreaking story is publicized throughout Iowa since the brothers are from Waterloo. Pictures of the five brothers appear in recruitment films and in posters appearing in

U.S. Post Offices throughout the United States. Mrs. Sullivan appears in newsreels and makes guest appearances on naval recruitment tours.

With every loss of life or major battle, Gene asks about his cousin's safety, "Is Francis OK?"

"Yes he's fine. He's in the United States, and he is learning how to repair army trucks and motor vehicles."

Gene frowns. He isn't fully aware of the training his cousin is receiving. It seems that he should be leaning how to be a soldier.

"You worry too much, Gene. Your cousin's OK," reassures his mother.

Hearing what he wants to hear, Gene joins his brothers in dressing warmly for their two mile walk to school. He struggles into his coat, pulls his stocking cap over his ears, tugs at the stubborn boots and stuffs his hands into his mittens. It's not below zero, but it is freezing and there is a slight wind blowing from the east.

"When a winter wind blows from the east snow is likely on its way," explains his dad. "If it is snowing when school lets out, I'll pick you up." The three boys don't waste any time but walk briskly in the early morning darkness arriving at school in a little over an hour.

The school is cold, and their breath can be seen once inside the school. The fire nearly burned out overnight, and Miss Frohling didn't get to school as early as usual. She is restarting the fire by stoking the coal embers with oak firewood. Soon a fire is roaring in the pot-belly stove, but it will be another half hour before it is warm enough to remove coats and caps.

She removes the construction paper snowflakes from the windows. Oh no, thinks Gene, it's another art day. While the three boys wait in the cold classroom wearing their coats, each boy is given a red sheet of construction paper.

"While we're waiting for the classroom to heat up, you can cut out Valentine hearts to decorate the windows," informs Miss Frohling. "Don't use a heart pattern. Just use your imagination and a pair of scissors to cut out a heart for the February window display."

This is easy, thinks Gene. I fold the paper, cut half a heart, unfold the paper, and there's a full heart. Just like Uncle Ed taught me. What Miss Frohling fails to tell Gene is that she doesn't want a crease down the middle of the paper. When she sees his heart, she gives Gene another sheet of paper and explains, "No wrinkles or creases, just a nice plain heart."

As students enter the classroom, they are given either a red or pink sheet of paper and instructed to cut out a heart. Gene's second heart looks terrible. It looks more like a real heart, like the one his Uncle Frank removed from a pig that he butchered last fall. One side is larger and there is no point at the bottom. To make the heart look less real, Gene trims one side trying to make it look balanced. The additional cutting results in scraps of red construction paper littering the floor and a very small heart.

Henry's heart is flawless. Cut from a pink sheet of construction paper, it has a perfect point. There is no doubt Henry's Valentine heart will be placed in the center of a window.

Henry makes fun of Gene's small lop-sided heart. "That'll fit nicely in a corner," he mocks.

Gene wants to hit him … right in the nose, but Mrs. Frohling approaches the two and instructs Gene to pick up the many scraps of red paper lying around his desk. The classroom is now warm, and Gene removes his outer winter garments and hangs them in the cloak room. He thinks to himself, If Henry left it would be the best day of my life.

The anticipated snow doesn't arrive during the day, so when school is dismissed the three boys, along with the three William sisters, begin their walk home. Iowa's winter sun sinks slowly in the West and the temperature begins to drop. Gene lags behind the others and pauses to warm up by lying down in the ditch. His oldest brother returns. "Get up and catch up," he tells Gene. "I don't want to get in trouble because you're lazy."

Slowly Gene stands up from the ditch. "You're walking too fast."

"We are not. You're walking too slow."

"I'm cold."

"You'll think cold if you don't get your butt in gear."

The rest of the students are a quarter mile ahead, and his brother runs to catch up with the others. Gene trudges forward, dragging his feet on the gravel road. The other students are now five minutes ahead of him, and the sun casts an orange, gray and blue coloring against the winter clouds as it sinks in the Western sky. Gene stops to admire the setting sun and then suddenly realizes it will soon be dark.

He begins to trot to catch up, but his buckle boots slow him down. The Williams have arrived at their homes, and his two brothers are at least a quarter of a mile ahead of him.

Gene plods up the long lane to his house and enters the kitchen door as the sun's orange -red glow surrenders to the evening's darkness.

"I'm home," shouts Gene wanting someone to miss him.

"I know," responds his mom. "Your brothers have been home for ten minutes. What took you so long?"

"The sunset," answers Gene.

"Well, you better take off your coat and place your gloves and boots near the stove, so they will be warm and dry tomorrow morning. Supper will be on the table in a few minutes."

Gene smells fried pork chops and fresh baking-powder biscuits. At six o'clock the family sits down to eat the pork and biscuits served with boiled potatoes, gravy made from the pork drippings, and green beans that were canned last summer. On the table is a jar of homemade apple butter and all the milk he can drink. The family gives thanks for food, the warm home, and a safe country. His mom adds a prayer for the Sullivan family.

Gene's dad has just returned from Farlin, a small village with about 40 residents. He was talking with Jack Johnson, a local trucker, who hauls hogs and cattle to the stockyard in the town of Churdan where buyers purchase livestock before shipping them in trains to Sioux City.

Farlin, like many small Iowa villages, is crumbling, but it was a promising town when Gene's dad grew up in the community. At that time there was a successful grain elevator, and the trains made scheduled stops. There was a bank which was once robbed according to his dad. The bank is now gone, along with a hotel and a restaurant that once prospered.

Scattered around Farlin are fully grown elm and box elder trees, providing shade to the homes. There remain two churches, one for the Baptists and another for those attending the Church of Christ. There is a two-room, two-story school. Lower elementary students attend classes on the first floor, and fifth through eighth grade students attend classes on the second floor. A post- office is attached to Mike's Food Market where locals buy flour, sugar, and Colonial bread. Also sold at Mike's are hardware items such as nails, wrenches, and farm tools. Most people in the community travel to Churdan or Jefferson for their weekly groceries and farm supplies, but many Bristol Township activities are held at the IOOF Hall.

Across the gravel road, on the south side, is a busy blacksmith shop. When the forge is fired up, black smoke belches from the outside vent. The blacksmith sharpens plow shares and mower blades and occasionally shoes a horse. Beside the blacksmith shop is a 'one table pool-hall' smelling of cigarette and cigar smoke where farmers play more cards than play eight-ball.

A block east of the blacksmith shop is the IOOF (Independent Order of Odd Fellow) Hall, which is in need of repair. The Odd Fellows hold their meeting in the large room and share their meeting space with the 4-H club and Farm Bureau members. Gene wants to meet an odd fellow and believes they must be strange men, but he isn't sure.

In the northeast corner of the town, the railroad stretches alongside a grain elevator that is in need of repair. Milligan is painted in large black letters near the top of the building, but the name has gradually faded over the years, and the last four letters, i-g-a-n, have almost disappeared. Gene pretends it reads Millard, Miller or just Mill. The elevator survived the 1930s Depression and some grain is still shipped out from Farlin, but there is no railroad depot.

A mixture of freight and passenger trains runs through the town, some trains carry coal from Angus and Waukee to Sioux City, others carry livestock or grain from area farmers to the stockyards in Sioux City, and a few trains transport people between Sioux City and Des Moines. Since the war, there is an increase in military personnel riding trains and an increase in the number of trains.

There are no scheduled stops at Farlin, but a person can board a train there. A ticket is purchased from a depot agent in another town, and on the day the person is to board the train the conductor stops the train to pick up the passenger. Persons catching a ride usually are traveling to a neighboring town between Sioux City and Des Moines. Behind the school is a community softball diamond, but following the war the diamond is moved to the north side of the railroad tracks. The softball field is where the 4-H club and the community softball team win and lose games while the farmers and wives exchange neighborhood gossip.

It's the card room that attracts most men to Farlin, and on rainy days and wintery afternoons farmers meet to share stories, play pitch, and tell lies. If Gene's dad has any spare time after farming, he is more likely to read a magazine than to play cards with the area farmers. He does go to the blacksmith to have plowshares sharpened and hires Jack Johnson to haul grain.

Gene bursts into the kitchen and shouts, "Henry's leaving, Henry's leaving." He shouts again, "Henry is leaving Iowa."

"Slow down, Gene, and tell us the story," his mother responds.

"Henry wasn't in school today. Miss Frohling told us he is moving to Toledo, Ohio. His dad is going to make Jeeps." Gene is delighted. Now he doesn't have to worry about Henry stealing his crayons or snooping in his desk.

His dad listens and then comments quietly, "Wars uproot families."

Gene looks at his dad suspiciously and asks, "How?"

"The war has caused neighbors and relatives to leave the small towns and move to the cities. They are working in factories and making airplanes, tanks, and guns; everything that is needed to beat the Nazis and the Japanese."

"Why don't the men in the cities do the work?" Gene asks.

"Men were outraged by the attack on Pearl Harbor and left to join the military service. Now men and women are moving to the cities to work as welders, lathe operators, and mechanics."

His dad is right. Everyone's life is affected. Two neighbor women moved to Waterloo, Iowa, to work at the John Deere Factory, producing aircraft parts and ammunition. Several young women from the Churdan Catholic Church took jobs at the Des Moines Ordnance Plant in Ankeny, Iowa, making ammunition for guns. Even his godmother, Annabelle, left Jefferson to work in Washington DC for the FBI after her brother Francis went into the Army. The Maytag factory in Newton, Iowa, stopped making washing machines and started making aircraft parts.

Gene's dad comments, "I've got some news, too."

"What?" inquires Gene?

"We're moving."

Gene doesn't say anything. He fears the family will be moving to Ankeny or Waterloo or Newton, so his dad can work in a war plant, or maybe to Toledo, Ohio. The war is interrupting everything. On a trip to Des Moines, Gene counted the rows of ammunition boxes piled high behind a barbwire fence outside the Ankeny ammunition plant. Soldiers were guarding the plant, and it made the war seem more real than the newsreels at the theater.

Maybe his dad was drafted.

"Are you drafted?" Gene asks his dad.

"Gene, we've discussed the draft, and I have not been drafted. I'm needed to farm and help feed the troops," answers his dad.

Relieved, Gene responds "Good," then looks skeptically at his dad and asks, "Then why are we moving?"

"We're moving to a better farm, and I asked Jack Johnson to help us move on March first.

"Can't we wait?"

"Farmers always move on March 1 to get ready for spring planting," his dad answers and then continues, "We're moving to a bigger and better farm; one hundred and sixty acres of good farm land. There are a few low areas that don't drain very well, but we can tile those. There's a pasture where I can raise a small dairy herd and feed up to seventy-five pigs. Your mother will be able to raise a hundred or more chickens."

"Will I go to a different school?"

"Yeah, you'll be going to a new school and making new friends." His dad returns to discussing their new home, "The house is larger, and there are three bedrooms. You and your younger brother will have your own bedroom. Your older brothers will have their bedroom."

"Will we have a bathroom?" Gene interrupts, thinking of his Uncle Frank's house in Jefferson that has both electricity and plumbing.

"Sorry son. We still won't have plumbing or electricity. But after the war the government will resume bringing electricity to the farms. We'll get electricity."

Trying to think of a reason why Gene might want to move he adds, "You won't have to walk two miles to school. Your new school is only an eighth of a mile from where we'll live."

Gene doesn't answer, but he isn't sure he likes the idea of leaving the pasture where he plays in the small creek and Bristol 7. And now that Henry is leaving school his life should improve. He would just as soon stay right here.

―――

A week later, on March 1, the entire family helps with the move. It is one of those rare days when the boys are excused from school. Mr. Johnson and Gene's dad load the kitchen range, a living room sofa, some chairs, an ice box, and several chests of drawers into a farm truck used for carrying livestock. They're thankful it is not raining or snowing, so there is no need to cover the furniture with a tarp. Boxes of home canned vegetables and fruit, along with kitchen utensils, are placed in the car. Gene's mom wraps dishes, which will be moved later. Gene's two older brothers carry boxes of clothes and linens to the truck. The truck and the car make several trips to the new farm.

"Get in the truck, and you can ride with Jack and me to see your new home." Gene's dad calls to him. Once they arrive Gene takes a brief tour of the six room house. It was originally a four room miner's style house with a kitchen, dining/living room and two bed rooms. Two additional bedrooms were added to the house, and one of the original bedrooms was converted to a parlor.

After being shown where he and his younger brother will sleep, Gene walks outdoors. South of the house is a large garden plot that is fenced off from a pasture. Further south is an unplowed field. West of the house is the weathered barn in need of painting and an empty corn crib. Beyond the barn is a grove of Catalpa trees with a few beans still hanging on. Catalpa trees are called bean trees and produce fragrant white flowers in the spring that become long beans that remain on the tree often throughout the winter. Some beans still dangle from the tree branches.

He spots a small marsh and pond north of the farm house. Beyond the marsh is the one room country school that he will attend. He can see a small separate cloakroom that is attached to the entrance of the school.

Gene looks more closely at the marsh and catches a glimpse of a muskrat swimming toward a small muskrat lodge built near the center of the marsh. The water is covered by a mixture of slushy ice and broken cattails, slough grass, and smashed fox tails. Gene smiles and thinks maybe this new place isn't so bad. It's a perfect place for him to search for turtles, snakes, or frogs and bring them to school, either for a science project or a mischievous prank.

The pond can serve as a gateway for his imagination. He can build a raft from discarded boards once the ice melts, and the marsh can become a setting for whatever he pleases. He may be Tom Sawyer floating with Huck Finn on the Mississippi or an American marine attacking the Japanese in an insect infested island in the South Pacific.

Looking at the shallow pond between his home and the school, he feels better. He returns to the house to hear his mom, "We won't be sleeping here tonight; let's go back to the Ulrich place and finish packing so we will be moved by tomorrow night. There is bread, homemade strawberry jam, and cookies in the kitchen cupboard for tomorrow's school lunches."

Before sunrise the family eats a breakfast of Corn Flakes and milk as Gene's dad packs the bed frames, mattresses, and the remaining kitchen supplies in the truck. His mother is eager to take possession of her new home but first must take the boys to their new school. Then she can attack and unpack the mountains of boxes, which were hauled yesterday.

With the school lunches in the car, she anxiously presses her sons, "Hurry; we don't want to be tardy in meeting your new teacher."

"Are you sure she knows we're coming?" asks Gene, thinking he might stay home another day and help his mother.

"Come on, you've already missed one day of school, and your new teacher, Miss Newman, is looking forward to meeting you and your brothers."

"I hope they have a globe," he warns her and then reveals, "I'm happy Henry isn't here."

"You worry too much," his mother replies as she hustles Gene out the door and into the car with his brothers.

They arrive at Bristol 2 also called the Stream's School. It is newer and larger than Bristol 7 and was built at the intersection of two gravel roads. Level farmland lies to the west and north of the school. In the northwest corner of the playground is an outhouse designated for boys, and in the northeast corner is the companion privy for girls. A half mile east of the school is the Hardin Creek, a stream where Gene will catch fish and learn to swim. South of the school is the marshy area between Gene's home and Bristol 2.

West of the schoolhouse on the school grounds is a storm cave, two squeaky swings, a teeter-totter, a lop-sided merry-go-round, and a grove of box elder and elm trees. The playground is larger than the one at his last school. It is half thawed and covered with elm branches broken off by winter ice storms and blown about by March winds. Gene envisions that in May it will come to life with quack-grass, dandelions, and fox tails.

The playground looks large enough to be the Wrigley's baseball field, which Gene knows only from his grandpa Harkins' stories. His grandfather was an amateur baseball player who was once offered a position with the Chicago Cubs. He never played with them, but remained in Iowa to farm. His grandfather has also bragged to Gene about the Notre Dame Football team. Gene knows little about football or Notre Dame, but he believes that this playground is large enough for any college team to play on. After the first measurable snowfall, the playground will be perfect for Fox and Geese, a game where students chase each other following circular trampled snow paths. He thinks to himself. This school has possibilities.

Gene gets out of the car and enters the cloak room with his mom and two brothers. The cloakroom is larger, but not unlike the one at his former school. Standing next to the drinking crock is a tall serious-looking woman dressed in a tailored two piece navy dress.

"I have been waiting for you and your sons," she begins, "I'm Miss Newman. Do you have the report cards from Miss Frohling?"

Gene studies the teacher's long brown hair that is tucked into a bun with a few loose strands of hair hanging over one ear. With her left hand she secures the runaway hair with a bobby pen, and with her right hand holds his report card. She quickly reviews his grades. Looking up she says, "All A's and B's. You must be a bright young man, Gene. But there's a B minus in art, so we will need to work on art projects."

Oh no, not more cutting out pictures, Gene thinks as he takes a quick glance at the kites cut from construction paper that decorate the windows.

"Come. Come, now. Sit next to Jimmy who will be completing his first year. He is a year younger than you."

Jimmy is wearing cowboy boots and a pair of Lee overalls. He is smaller than Gene and has dark hair and playful brown eyes. He grins mischievously. Gene wants to ask him if he eats crayons and glue but reconsiders and replies with, "Hi," before sliding into his assigned seat.

———

After his first day at Bristol 2, Gene dashes home to help unpack the boxes piled high on the kitchen table and on the back porch. All the furniture is inside the house, and the wood burning kitchen stove pipe is connected to the outside chimney. A soft wood fire is burning in the stove, providing sufficient heat to remove the March chill from the room, and the aroma of beef and vegetable soup fills the house. The bed frames are assembled with mattresses placed on the springs, and a dresser has been placed in each bedroom, but the sheets are missing and the clothes need to be stored in the dressers.

"You can unpack your clothes and arrange them in your dresser," directs his mom.

Gene begins to whine, "The boxes are too heavy for me."

"If they are too heavy take the clothes out of the box and carry them one piece at a time."

Realizing it will be easier to move the box Gene pushes and pulls the box full of clothes into the back bedroom, which he will share with his younger brother. Gene isn't careful stuffing his shirts, underwear, overalls, and socks into the top two drawers of the four drawer dresser, and then he crams his younger brother's clothes into the bottom two drawers.

His mom joins him in the bedroom and unfolds the bed sheets that have been dried outdoors. The freshness permeates the room. "Only sheets dried outside can smell that refreshing," his mom says.

Once the sheets and blankets are in place, she centers the crazy quilt bedspread on the wrought-iron bed. The bedspread was made by Gene's grandmother during the Depression from worn-out clothes. He loves the name of the quilt as much as he likes examining the multi-colored fabric. It was used on his parent's bed until his mom replaced it with a new chenille bedspread decorated with pink flowers. Now the crazy quilt decorates his bedroom.

The smell of hot beef vegetable soup, the fragrance of fresh bed sheets, and the comfort of seeing the crazy quilt with its frayed patches reassures the six year old that this is home.

"How did your day at school go?" asks Gene's mom.

"OK, I met a new kid."

"Who's that?"

"Jimmy."

"Maybe you and he will be friends."

"We didn't talk much. He wears cowboy boots, and he likes cowboy movies. He especially likes Roy Rogers." Gene is pleased since Gene Autry can remain his favorite cowboy without sharing him with someone else.

"Our teacher says that Friday she is selling war saving stamps. Can I buy a stamp?" asks Gene. He then adds, "What is a war saving stamp?"

His mother explains, "The US Government encourages everyone to buy war bonds. When $18.50 worth of stamps is glued in your booklet, there is enough to obtain a war bond, a US Savings Bond. The government uses the money to buy weapons to fight the war, and ten years later the government pays you back $25.00."

This isn't the first time Gene has heard of US Saving Bonds. Posters of women working in war plants, men fighting in battles, and Uncle Sam promoting war bonds are seen throughout Greene County. There is even a poster in Gene's new school of two boys and a girl standing on a grass lawn under the shadow of a swastika. Under the picture is printed: *Don't Let That Shadow Touch Them - Buy War Bonds.*

The United States Government encourages children to buy "US War Bonds" and Miss Newman, along with teachers throughout the United States, sell war stamps in schools. Some schools hold contests, rewarding those who buy the most stamps. With limited cash in post Depression rural Iowa, the students in one-room schools are encouraged to buy stamps only when they afford them. There are no contests at Bristol 2. Saving ten cents a month is not easy, and it takes one hundred and eighty-five dimes to buy $18.50 worth of stamps. There's no dime for Gene to take to school on Friday. The following month Gene receives a half dollar for his seventh birthday on April 6, 1943, from his Aunt Leona.

"What are you going to buy?" asks his mother.

"I'm going to help end the war and buy some war stamps," Gene pledges.

On Friday I am bringing my half dollar to school to buy stamps."

"You may want to save some money for a movie," suggests his mom.

Gene weighs the decision and opts to buy only three stamps. On Thursday night his mom exchanges his half dollar for five dimes. Gene saves two dimes and takes three to school.

As he dashes off to school, his mom calls out, "Don't lose your money." Hearing her advice, he buries the dimes in the top front pocket of his Oshkosh bib overalls.

When Miss Newman asks, "Who is buying stamps?" Gene proudly walks to her desk and produces three dimes in exchange for three stamps. She gives him a United States treasure department booklet provided by the Greene County School Superintendent. Gene licks the stamps and carefully sticks them in the booklet. He then places the booklet with the three stamps in his top pocket and snaps the pocket shut. He feels he is doing something to end the war and knows his contribution will keep those evil Nazis from coming to this country.

Gene likes his new friend Jimmy, and he no longer worries about Henry bugging him. Jimmy is a lot different than Henry. Jimmy enjoys playing cowboy and Indian, and they sometimes argue as to who is braver – Roy Rogers or Gene Autry. They reenact western movies in the marsh located between the school and Gene's home and from time to time bicker as to who will play cowboy and who will be the Indian. Gene often volunteers to be the Indian, so he can hide in the tall marsh grass and unexpectedly attack his friend. Attacking from undercover is something that neither Rogers nor Autry would ever do because they must follow their codes of conduct. Respected cowboys must confront their opponents openly and directly.

Another of their shared interests is going to the movies. Two of their favorite movies are *The Flying Tigers* starring John Wayne and *Wake Island* telling about the Japanese attack on that island. The movies stimulate their interest in war, and they recreate "hand to hand" combat in the marsh with the Japanese Imperial Army. After they reenact the battle scenes, they return home wet and covered with slough grass and often receive a scolding for being so muddy.

To avoid getting too dirty, they change their reenactments to the edge of the swamp. Sidestepping the slimy marsh water, they encounter undergrowth sections of ragweed, wild carrot, and patches of bull thistles. The most effective way to cut through the undergrowth is to use field corn knives which resemble the machetes used by Marines fighting in the jungles. The large knives are stored in the barn and are only to be used for field work like cutting sunflowers and cocklebur from the corn.

When combat machetes are needed the boys secretly remove two knives, play with them in the marsh, and carefully return them to the barn after their jungle battles. Being sneaky is something real cowboys would never do, but it is excused if you're fighting the Nazis or the Japanese. Not getting caught only tempts them to become more devious.

Throughout the summer of 1943, the two boys recreate numerous movie scenes. Their reenactments are based on the propaganda portraying dull stupid Germans and Japanese with buck teeth, yellow skin, and slanted eyes. Their comic books – *Superman*, *The Green Lantern*, and *Captain America* – often encourage feelings that are anti-German and anti-Japanese. *Wonder Woman*, a hero who wages war against evil, is designed to be a model for girls, but they enjoy reading about her adventures as much as they enjoy *Captain America*.

Gene reads the comics as best he can and listens to the radio programs like *Jack Armstrong the All American Boy*, *Captain Midnight*, *The Green Hornet*, and *The Shadow*. The radio programs also depict the Germans and Japanese as hostile and menacing. A steady diet of war propaganda is not good for impressionable seven and eight year old boys.

In early November 1943 the cold weather forces the two to retreat to the hay loft to play their war games. They continue to protect the people in Greene County. However, their mothers become spies in checking on their whereabouts and their behavior.

"What are you two doing up there?" Jimmy's mom calls to the boys from the ladder leading to the barn's hay loft.

"Making a fort," both boys answer at once

"What kind of fort?"

"One that will keep us safe if the Nazis attacked our country," Gene answers.

"We're not under attack, and our soldiers are winning this war. You don't have to worry," Jimmy's mother responds, hoping to provide some adult reasoning.

"You never know, but with these corn knives we can take out a few before they get us." Jimmy responds.

"What do you mean – corn knives?"

Knowing they've said too much, they don't answer.

Jimmy's mother peeks into the hay loft from the top of the ladder. Resting on a plank are two large corn knives and a World War I bayonet that the boys found in the work shed. A stack of *Captain America* comic books rests beside the weapons. "Well?" Jimmy's mom asks not needing to ask the full question.

"Mom," Jimmy pleads, "the Nazis and even the Jap's are planning on invading us. The Japs attacked Hawaii, and the German's have submarines off the East Coast of the United States. It says so in these comic books. We've got to be ready."

"No knives," his mother declares as she confiscates them and grabs the comic books. "Both of you will explain this to your dads."

Gene walks home slowly, and he quietly enters the back door leading to the kitchen. His mom is mending socks at the kitchen table. The telephone rings – three long rings and one short ring, number thirty-one. That is Gene's family number, and although he doesn't know who is calling, he suspects it is Jimmy's mom. Gene's mom answers the phone.

She doesn't say much, mostly yes, no, yes, no, yes.

Finally she replies, "Thanks for calling."

She hangs up the phone, turns, and glares at Gene, "That was Jimmy's mom. We'll talk about 'this' with your dad. You had better do your chores."

He does a particularly thorough job of feeding the pigs. Normally he dumps the ears of corn into the feeding trough, and if some tumble outside he doesn't worry. The pigs will find them. Tonight he makes sure each ear of corn ends up in the trough. He even scratches the backs of some of the larger pigs. He avoids going to the house. He is worrying about what his parents will do about the knives. A chore that usually takes fifteen minutes takes a half hour. As the supper hour approaches, he knows he can't postpone the punishment.

Supper is on the table and his parents say nothing; he takes his place at the table. His brothers ask questions about the relocation of the 110,000 Japanese-Americans that are being talked about on the radio.

Gene isn't interested in talking, and when everyone has finished eating he jumps up and volunteers to wash the dishes.

His mother looks at him and says, "Not so fast, young man, we need to talk." The waiting is over.

"How could you be so irresponsible?" questions his mom.

Before he can answer, his dad asks, "What were you thinking? You know you are not to play with the corn knives."

"I wasn't thinking," answers Gene, "and it was Jimmy's dad's knives."

"You could have hurt someone," snaps his mom.

"I'm sorry. What can I do?" Gene answers.

"First, promise not to mess around with knives, especially those machetes. They are used only in the fields."

"OK."

"Second, stop reading those dumb comic books."

"All of them? Gene cries, "What about Archie?"

His mom answers firmly, "No comics."

"You're more interested in looking at comic books and listening to radio program than in doing your homework. From now until Christmas, you can only listen to the radio programs we approve. No listening to *The Shadow* or *The Green Hornet*. Thanksgiving is approaching and you can listen to *Cinnamon Bear*.

Gene was first introduced to the popular 1940s children's radio program, *Cinnamon Bear*, last year after. His mother believes that the 1939 movie, *The Wizard of Oz*, encouraged radios to find a fantasy program that would compete with the movie. *Cinnamon Bear* met that challenge and she hopes the fifteen minute radio broadcast will divert Gene's attention away from the war. The twenty-six episodes are based around a fantasy and broadcast every year from Thanksgiving until Christmas Eve.

Between Thanksgiving and the beginning of Christmas vacation, Gene runs home from school jumping over frozen water spots on the gravel road, to listen to the latest adventure. Pushing open the front door he throws his coat in a corner and turns on the radio to listen to the fantasy characters in Maybeland. He looks forward to discovering where Paddy O'Cinnamon, the small teddy-like bear, and the Crazy Quilt Dragon will fly Judy and Jimmy on the magic carpet. The four radio characters are searching for the Silver Star that has been stolen from the children's attic. They encounter a giant, a witch, a rabbit that speaks in rhymes, pirates, and the Crazy Quilt Dragon who hinders their search as much as helps them in finding the star. At the closing of each day's program, an anxious situation arises that will need to be resolved the following afternoon. At school Gene and Jimmy exchange insights as to where Paddy might lead them in the search.

His mother's plan to distract Gene's interest away from the war works. He becomes more interested as to where the Crazy Quilt Dragon will find the Silver Star than in playing war games. On December 24 the star is placed atop Judy and Jimmy's Christmas tree and the radio program is over for another year.

Gene's family enjoys a traditional oyster soup supper and celebrates in front of a three foot cedar tree by opening gifts. The tree is decorated with the same glass pine cones, balls and acorn ornaments that were used last year and tinsel, which has been recycled the past five years. The meager looking cedar has a papier-mâché angel placed at the top of the tree.

Gene and his brothers impatiently open their gifts that wait under the tree: a model airplane for his oldest brother, a book for his other brother and clothes for his youngest brother. Gene receives an autograph book.

Autograph books have existed since the nineteenth century and were generally filled with poems and verses written by girls to girls. In the early twentieth century these books lost their popularity, but returned in the 1930s and 40s. The renewed interest may have resulted because of the Great Depression and World War II, which limited toys to children, or maybe the books returned because of the melancholy and despondent atmosphere of the war years. The war is now starting its third year and has taken a toll on people's emotions. Everyone is seeking a return to more cheerful times.

Gene's mother's motive for having him listening to *Cinnamon Bear* and giving him the autograph book is clear-cut. She wants to find peaceful activities for him and keep him more interested in non-violent games.

1944

A light snow fell overnight, covering the muddy reminders of last week's thaw. Gene stomps his feet on the school's pine wood floor to remove the snow from his boots, shakes the snow off his cap, and swings around in the chilly cloakroom. It looks like a happy dance, but it's a way for him to keep warm and remove the snow from his clothing. He carefully places the small green autograph book on the shelf next to his lunch. He takes off his coat, hangs it on a peg, and leans against the wall to remove his four buckle overshoes.

Picking up the book, he walks proudly into the classroom. Students are gathered in the rear of the classroom near the coal burning stove. They are exchanging vacation stories and are excited about the Johnson's new Flexible Flyer sled and Barbara's "Claudette Colbert" paper doll set. Gene shows them his autograph book and asks them to write whatever they like in the book. There is little interest in the small book.

"How fast do you think the sled will go?" Jimmy asks Bill Johnson.

"Fastest sled I've ever seen," replies Bill. "Dad says the Flexible Flyers are the best."

"Where did they find it?" chimes in Larry.

"Don't know, must have been one left over from before the war," answers Bill. "I suppose they found it in the Fort Dodge Coast to Coast hardware store. They have everything there."

"See, both my brothers have written in my book," interrupts Gene. "You can write anywhere in it. My mom wrote here on the first page."

> Jan. 1, 1944
> Dearest Son,
> The ocean is wide.
> The sea is deep.
> The Ten Commandments
> Be sure to keep.
> Mother

"And my dad also wrote something," Gene says hoping someone will ask to look at his book.

> January 1, 1944
> Remember to always
> Be honest and true
> And all good things
> In life will come to you.
> Your Dad

Gene cares little about what the students might write; he just wants someone to write something. No one is interested, but then how could an autograph book compete with a new Flexible Flyer? He stops at Miss Newman's side as she shovels another scoop of coal into the round-bellied stove. He asks quietly, "Will you sign my autograph book?"

"I'll be happy to write in your book, and I'll leave it on my desk since some of the students may want to write later."

"Thanks," Gene responds. She writes on the last page of the book.

> Jefferson, Iowa
> January 3, 1944
> Dear Gene
> Away back here out of sight,
> I'll sign my name just
> for spite.
> Your teacher,
> Miss Betty Newman

At the end of the day Gene picks up the book and smiles: several students wrote in his book. Carol, who often wears a dress with a slight flare and a flowery pattern, is the only student in eighth grade. She has long goldilocks curls and a pretty smile and helps Gene practice the Palmer writing exercises to improve his hand coordination. He hates the exercise as much as he hates cutting, but he likes Carol and she has written a poem in flawless penmanship:

> January 3, 1944
> I love the cornfield in the fall,
> With all the rustling cornstalks tied
> In tall gray wigwams everywhere.
> They make the nicest places to hide.
> But of course that is gone now.
> But it will come around again next fall.
> Carol

After several erasures his friend Jimmy prints:

> Roses are red
> Violets are blue
> Kids that's mean
> Are made into glue
> Jimmie
> Drop dead twice
> I don't really mean it Ha, Ha.

Barbara had a different view of the roses verse:

> Roses are red
> Violets are blue.
> Monkeys like you
> Belong in the zoo.
> Barbara

Nancy, who is in sixth grade, didn't write anything. She wears overalls and likes to play baseball with the guys, and probably thinks autograph books are only for sissies.

Gene flips through the pages looking for other poems; finding none he is happy that goofy Nancy was absent. She would have probably written a love poem.

Bill, Larry and Nancy leave Bristol 2 in March; but two new students, Vincent and his sister Marilyn, transfer in. Vincent is younger than Gene, smaller, and wants involved in everything that Gene and Jimmy undertake. His older sister Marilyn is skinny and wears dresses made of flour sacks. They bring their lunch in a metal syrup pail. Every day their lunch is the same; two lard sandwiches and two hard boiled eggs. Gene returns with his autograph book and asks them to sign it. Vincent only prints his name, but Marilyn prints:

> Gene
> When you get married
> And live across the river
> Butcher a cat and
> Send me the liver
> Marilyn

For the remainder of the year Gene collects autographs and poems from students who were reluctant to write in his book in January. He decides that sometimes people do things in private that they won't do in front of others.

―――

Since the Alamo holdout in Jimmy's hayloft, Gene hasn't been thinking much about the war. His mother credits her plot of having him listening to the *Cinnamon Bear* radio program and giving him the autograph book for lessening his interest in war games. She hopes that since he is not reading the comic books he will concentrate on school assignments. But there are no signs that the war will be over soon, and she can't continue to isolate him from the war. There are signs of combat, battles and war efforts everywhere.

Gene has fears about what is happening to his cousin Francis, especially after seeing a war movie. There is a small flag with a red border, white background, and blue star that hangs in the front window of his Uncle Frank's home, and it is a lone reminder of his cousin. Each time Gene visits his uncle's house he examines the flag closely and thinks of Francis fighting in the war. He wishes Francis was there to mess up his hair and say, "If it isn't Eugene the Jeep?" Gene dislikes being compared to the character with a large nose that looks something like a dog. Even if Eugene the Jeep has magical powers and appears in the Popeye comic strips, it's not flattering to be called Eugene the Jeep; nevertheless, he does miss the attention given to him by his cousin. Horsing around makes Gene feel important, like when Francis returned from boot camp last December, and he and his brothers had a snowball fight.

Gene notices that other homes have flags displayed in their front windows. "Why do some flags have blue stars and some have gold stars?" Gene asks his dad.

"A blue star means that someone in the house is serving in the United States military. If there are two stars, there are two people serving, and if the star is gold the person was killed."

Gene counts fifteen flags appearing in houses in Bristol Township, an area of thirty-six square miles. The flags represent soldiers, sailors, and army pilots from neighboring families who are serving in World War II.

Gene and his dad venture to Farlin to have Charlie, the blacksmith, sharpen plowshares for spring plowing. Gene is fascinated by the bellows that pump air into the forge. Charlie lets him pull the bellow's rope that forces air into the forge causing the coal to burn a white flame. While Gene swings on the bellow's rope, Charlie and Gene's dad discuss the war.

Charlie boasts, "My brother's son, who was drafted, was home last week. He told me that from now on all soldiers will be trained to fight the

Japanese since Germany is ready to surrender. It's pretty near top secret, so he didn't tell his mother. He doesn't want her to worry, you know."

"I'm surprised he even told you," replies Gene's dad. "Soldiers and sailors are to keep quiet about what they hear. Like the posters say, 'Loose Lips Sink Ships.' And we have lots of young men from Bristol who are fighting to bring peace to this world."

"Well, be sure not to tell anyone," cautions Charlie.

Gene's dad shifts the topic, "Do you know if there is going to be a metal drive next Saturday?"

"Think so. They're collecting tin, scrap iron, copper, and aluminum down at Jefferson."

Gene and his dad exit the sweaty blacksmith shop, taking with them the stench of smelted iron, and walk toward the post office to buy some postage stamps. A notice confirms that there is a scrap drive in Jefferson, and a poster encourages everyone to save old rubber, paper, rags, engine grease and even kitchen fat. The grease and fat are used in making ammunition. Children are encouraged to save the tin foil from cigarette and gum packages and bring the items to community scrap drives. Scrap drives help people in communities feel that they are helping to defeat the enemy while keeping the war foremost in the public's mind.

Another poster, which Charlie must have not read, shows Uncle Sam with a finger to his lips, the poster reads – *I'm Counting on You. Don't Discuss: Troop Movements, Ship Sailing, and War Equipment.* The members of the community accept the responsibility to do what they can to end the war, but they do complain about the national speed limit of 35 miles per hour.

Mike at the Food Market comments, "If the government wants me to conserve gasoline and rubber, let me drive faster, and I won't be on the road as long." Gene and his dad leave the store with the men laughing at one another's wise cracks.

At home Gene collects a few old metal toys and places the metal in a cardboard box after cutting off the rubber tires which he stores in a glass fruit jar. On Saturday's trip to Jefferson, he smugly carries the box and the jar to the civilian defense worker who is collecting rubber and metal. The volunteer throws the metal toys on top of the huge scrap pile and tosses the rubber items into a US Army dumpster truck.

Returning the box and jar he says, "Here's a penny for your contributions. With patriots like you, this war will end before Christmas."

During the summer of 1944 Gene's time is divided between riding with his Uncle Ed on produce routes, fishing with his friend Jimmy, and following the progress of the war in *The Des Moines Register*.

Gene's Aunt Beulah dies unexpectedly of childbirth on June 11, 1944, only five days after the invasion of Normandy, leaving a three year old daughter to be raised by her husband. Her husband is Gene's Uncle Ed who is part owner of the C and M Produce in Jefferson, Iowa. On occasion Gene or his brothers ride with their uncle to pick up eggs at farms around Greene County. The rides are a welcomed relief from the Iowa summer heat, and Gene learns excuses for the Iowa weather from farmers telling him that, "It's not the heat; it's the humidity" or "The humidity is good for the corn."

On the days that Gene doesn't go for a ride with his uncle he waits by the mail box for the paper to arrive. On some days Jimmy joins him, not to read the paper but to entice Gene to go fishing.

While the two friends wait for the newspaper to arrive beads of sweat trickling down their suntanned backs. Jimmy becomes restless and suggests they go fishing at Hardin Creek.

Gene is more interested in looking at the maps that will be in the paper, "Before I go fishing I've got to see how far the American and British troops have advanced in France."

The two boys continue to hang around the roadside. Jimmy picks a couple of hollyhocks that grow near the mailbox and throws them at

Gene, who is sitting on his heels. Gene ignores him and at 10:30 am the carrier drives up in his black 1934 Ford and tosses the paper to Gene.

"Sorry I'm late. I had to wait for gas this morning. This gas rationing is causing me lots of headaches."

Gene catches the paper, rises from his squatting position, and the two boys walk quickly to the house. Opening the kitchen screen door, Gene announces, "We've got another map to study."

Gene has faithfully followed *The Des Moines Register's* World War II maps, and in doing so he learns of places in Northern Europe like: Normandy, Belgium, Denmark, Norway, Sweden and of the Southern European countries of Italy, Spain, and Yugoslavia. He is always interested in the Russian advances on the Eastern Front and follows the Allies' movements in France. There are news stories about the invasion of Sicily, the surrender of the Italian Army, and the Germans' battle for Stalingrad that kills nearly two million people before the Russian Army begins to push the German Army back to Germany.

Kneeling on the seats of white painted chairs, he and Jimmy spread the new map over a worn table cloth stenciled with strawberries and strawberry vines. The two begin to study the map and make comments.

"We're getting close to Paris."

"Where's Patton's army?"

"I hope we're fighting better than those Russians?"

And Gene's daily question, "Have the Allies reached Alsace Lorraine?"

Gene's dad has told him that the Millard name is believed to have come from this northeast region of France that borders Germany and Belgium. He tells Gene that his ancestors came from the area and the area has been fought over for years. It first belonged to Germany, then France, and continues to be fought over by the two rivals.

Jimmy believes the maps are more factual about the geography than about military advances, and comments, "You don't think General Eisenhower is going to tell us what he's doing?"

Gene's interest in the war is becoming personal since his godfather and uncle, Martin Harkins who lives in Chicago, is drafted in June 1944. Gene remembers him from his visits to Iowa to go pheasant hunting. The visits have been less frequent the past few years, but like Francis, his godfather makes him feel special.

Uncle Mart always asks to see a scar on Gene's forehead, a scar Gene received after falling off his uncle's lap while riding in a car. When Gene fell, he cut his forehead on a heater switch. Gene enjoys the attention and tells his uncle it doesn't hurt anymore.

"Come on, Gene. Enough of the map," shouts Jimmy as he leaves the kitchen. "Let's go fishing."

"Maybe tomorrow. I don't feel like fishing today. I got to do some thinking." answers Gene.

"You can think while we're fishing."

"I don't want to fish. Didn't you hear me?"

As he heads home for lunch Jimmy shouts back over his shoulder, "You don't have to bite my head off."

The war is beginning to dominate Gene's thoughts, and after watching the D-day invasion newsreel and the landings on the Omaha, Utah, and JUNO beaches he is concerned about his cousin and his godfather. Maybe the war isn't going as well as everyone says. Maybe the war with the Nazis will not be over by Christmas. Maybe the maps are wrong. His mother doesn't even believe Uncle Mart will be sent to Europe. She says he is more likely to go to the Pacific and fight the Japanese.

After the disagreement with Jimmy, Gene quizzes his mother, "Where's Uncle Mart?"

"He's completing his training in Florida. Don't worry, Gene," his mom assures him. "This war will be over by the time he completes his basic training."

"Where's Francis?"

"The last we heard, he's in England."

"I hope so," says Gene, but he isn't convinced.

The following week at the July fourth family picnic, he hears his mom and Aunt Leona talking.

"Even after the Nazis' surrender there will be lots of fighting in the Pacific," his mom comments.

"And the Japanese Empire is going to be difficult to defeat," replies his aunt.

The following day Gene is thinking that the war may go on for years; he strolls along the marshy pond north of the house. There he practices war tactics; after all he may have to become a soldier. He climbs aboard his makeshift raft of scrap timber and pretends it's an imaginary landing craft. His dog Laddie jumps aboard, and Gene, using a long pole maneuvers the raft to the middle of the shallow pond. Slowly he and his loyal four-legged companion approach the opposite side of the pond. Hiding behind small willow bushes, cattails, wild hemp, and milkweeds, they spy on the school that is serving as the headquarters of the Nazis Military Panzer Division. Cautiously, the two wade through the cattails as bombs explode around them. It isn't much of an enactment: Gene is without a shirt, bare footed, and carrying a tree branch that resembles a rifle.

Nevertheless, he bravely crawls through the weeds and quickly climbs over the wire fence, pretending it is a Normandy Hedgerow. Without the help of one US Sherman tank, he and his capable military dog capture the one-room school, which houses the entire Nazi headquarters staff. Somehow playing at war makes him feel he is helping to win the war.

In the summer of 1944 nearly all of the families rationed sugar is used before the peaches arrive. There are still apples to can, and apple butter and apple sauce to make for winter. His mom examines the family's ration books and concludes there wouldn't be enough sugar for all of the canning.

The Office of Price Administration (OPA) issues ration books for meat, sugar, coffee, and even shoes; it started about six months after the war began and still continues. His dad believes rationing will continue even after the war is over. There are ration books for gasoline and tires, but farmers are provided additional gasoline.

Each family member is issued a ration book with stamps for specific items. The stamps in the books are good for a stated period of time, and when the stamps expire new ration books are issued. The newspapers publish information explaining when the new booklets will be made available. When buying rationed items at stores, Gene's mom removes stamps from the ration books and gives them to the grocery store proprietor. The rationing of meat is less of a problem for farmers since they often butcher their own hogs. Limiting coffee doesn't bother either his mom or dad; they drink less. However, the rationing of sugar annoys Gene's mom.

The rationing system limits the amount of rationed items to the public, provides equal distribution, and keeps prices under control since store owners are to charge a stated price. In addition it makes the public aware of the seriousness of the war, and warnings are posted in stores about obeying the rationing regulations and avoiding the black market for purchasing items.

"We're nearly out of sugar stamps," Gene's mom complains. "And we still have peaches, cherries, and apples to can."

"On our next trip to Fort Dodge, we'll stop at the railroad station," whispers his dad.

"Do you think we should? You know it's illegal."

"Everyone is doing it, and the sugar they are selling is from American sugar beets raised right here in the good old USA. It isn't like we are taking sugar away from the war effort. And I heard Mike at Farlin say that the U. S. Government is actually keeping sugar off the market."

The following week the family drives to Fort Dodge to purchase shoes, overalls, and winter shirts for school. The Fort Dodge stores have a larger selection of clothing stores than Jefferson, and there's the mysterious railroad station. Leaving Fort Dodge, Gene's dad takes a different route home, turning down a gravel road to a railroad turnout. He slows to a stop alongside a cargo car that is concealed behind a grove of pine trees. Gene's dad strolls quietly over to the cargo car as if he doesn't want to frighten pheasants hiding in the tall grass. An overweight man crawls out of the railroad car, removes his cap, and scratches a bald spot on his head. "Can I help you sir?" asks the surly looking worker.

"Sure."

The two men enter the railroad car. Several minutes later Gene's dad re-emerges, carrying a large white sack. He places the sack in the front seat next to Gene's mom. The only thing Gene hears from his dad is, "It's too damn expensive."

Gene returns to school September 4, 1944, and enters the third grade. Miss Newman left their school, and the new teacher is Miss Crowley. There is a stack of gunny sacks or burlap bags in the cloak room, and Mr. Morris, the county school superintendent, is seated next to the teacher's desk. After the Pledge of Allegiance Miss Crowley asks, "How many of you collected scrap iron this past summer?" All raise their hands. "Well, there is something else we can collect to help end the war."

Mr. Morris, sporting a big smile, stands and announces, "Our country is running low on rubber and kapok,"

"What's kapok?" asks Jimmy.

"It's a light cotton-like fiber that comes from the Ceiba tree in Malay, and is very important for sailors and pilots because the fiber doesn't absorb water. It's used in manufacturing life jackets," he explains. "The Japanese Navy is sinking our merchant ships, and the United States can't depend on a kapok supply from the Pacific."

"We collected old rubber," responds Jimmy, "but we can't collect kapok unless we swim the Pacific." Everyone laughs.

"But we can help," replies Mr. Morris. "The United States scientists have found a kapok substitute."

"Don't laugh now, but guess what they are using in place of kapok for life jackets? Milkweed pods!" he said, answering his own question. "Well, not really the pods, but the milkweed's floss that is inside the pods. And all of you have the opportunity to help in the war effort by collecting pods this week."

"You'll go in teams of two," explains Miss Crowley and urges the students to, "Pick as many pods as possible. Our sailors need life jackets."

Gene and Jimmy immediately form a team, and after lunch head for the marsh across from the school. The tall grass catches on their belts as they walk the marsh. The dry autumn air is full of goldenrod pollen, causing both boys to sneeze. They return to the school with a full burlap bag in less than thirty minutes, and there are still hundreds of milkweed pods surrounding the marsh and plenty more in the ditches.

"Do you think these silly pods will really help win the war?" asks Gene, whose eyes are becoming red from pollen.

"I sure hope so," replies Jimmy. "We can't just sit and wait for the war to end."

"Maybe we should leave some milkweeds pods," Gene comments

"Why."

"There needs to be some pods left, so there will be milkweeds next year."

"You must be thinking about food for the butterflies?"

"Yeah, it's fun seeing the marsh full of Monarchs."

By the end of the week, the students have collected over a dozen bags of milkweed pods for Mr. Morris to pickup. And although their backs ache, their eyes sting, and their hands throb the students feel good about helping. That night Gene is extra careful not to burst the puffy soft blisters on his hands. He is proud of doing something that really might help his uncle and cousin. And he is proud that Jimmy and he filled more sacks with milkweed pods than any other team.

Since the Normandy invasion, *The Des Moines Register's* maps show the Allied forces making daily advances to liberate Paris and then on to free the "Millard's homeland" around the Alsace Lorraine region. According to his dad, the Nazis are retreating to Berlin like "a bat out of hell." This year the family is looking forward to enjoying a good-news Christmas.

At the Thanksgiving dinner, Gene enjoys wild pheasant and goose, stuffing, mashed potatoes, sweet potatoes, peas, pumpkin pie, and mince-meat pie served in a thankful atmosphere at his Aunt Leona and Uncle Virgil's farm. There is much discussion about the war in Europe and most of the relatives believe it will to be over soon. According to recent stories, the German Army is retreating or surrendering. The family has heard that Uncle Mart is headed for Europe and will arrive sometime before Christmas, just in time to see the Nazis surrender.

Following Christmas, there are rumors about a German offense into Belgium. The battle lines that had been moving toward Germany since the Normandy invasion are now bending backward causing a bulge in the battle lines toward France and Belgium. After reviewing the maps and reading the news stories Gene's dad believes that the Alsace area, which has been fought over by the Germans and French, is again being targeted, and it appears to be back under German control. This recent battle casts a cloud over the 1944 Holiday Season, and the hope for an early end to the war has vanished.

For Christmas Gene is eyeing the airplane models that young boys make from balsa wood and tissue paper. There are Hellcats, Thunderbolts, P-38s, B-17, or B24s, and he receives a P-38 airplane model under the Christmas tree. His skills are limited, and after the basic framework of the plane is cut out and glued he never completes covering the balsa-wood skeleton with tissue paper. The decals for his model plane that include stars for the wings, frightening eyes and teeth decals for the nose of the plane, are stuck to his comic books, on barn doors, and in his school text books.

His favorite 1944 Christmas gift is a cut-out cardboard airplane cockpit, equipped with movable dials and an aviator's cap with goggles. He wears the cap to school, to town on Saturday afternoons, church on Sunday mornings, and always when he's playing. He and his new cap are inseparable.

1945

"I can hardly see the map," Gene complains to his mother as he reviews today's newspaper war map with older maps he keeps under his bed. The kerosene lamp flickers, creating shadows across the kitchen table, making it difficult to read the maps.

"Just a minute, I'll light the Aladdin Lamp," his mom replies.

Gene goes to the kitchen cabinet, stands on a chair, and hands down a box with an Aladdin mantle in it. The lamp doesn't have a plain wick, but instead an oblong half globe mantle that absorbs the kerosene and mixes it with the air to provide a blue flame. His mother lights the Aladdin lamp and snuffs out the other lamp. The new soft white light brightens the entire kitchen. Gene can easily read the maps with the new lighting and sees that the allied forces have stopped moving. Nor is there any movement with the German armies.

Gene's dad reviews the map with Gene and then predicts, "It isn't going to end as quickly as we had hoped."

"Sometimes the newspapers don't report the full story. I wonder what is really happening," adds his mother.

"For sure the Nazis want to stop the Americans from entering Germany, and their counterattack near the Belgium border proves it," responds Gene's dad as he points to the Alsace Lorraine area in northeast France. That is the geographical area where the Millard name is thought to come from.

"I hope Uncle Mart isn't there," Gene says, wishing that his mom or dad knew where his uncle was stationed.

Neither his mom nor dad comments because they don't know. The last they heard he was heading for Europe and not the Pacific as they had earlier thought.

"It's getting late, better hustle to bed, Gene," directs his mom. "Christmas vacation is over, and it's back to school tomorrow morning."

She relights the kerosene wick lamp sitting on the wash stand, and they both enter the unheated bedroom. The lamp's flickering creates wobbly shadows on the walls as Gene quickly and quietly undresses. He leaves his long johns on to provide additional warmth under the crazy quilt bedspread and buries himself in the featherbed beneath the blankets. As his mom leaves, her shadow dances haphazardly, creating a dark unsteady image like an injured soldier looking for a place to hide.

Gene listens to the northern wind rage outside and spit ice against the bedroom window. The dislodged ice raps on the window making a sound like a lost bird pecking at the window in search of a safe haven. Gene turns his back to the window and whispers his prayers before falling asleep, "God bless the soldiers in the war, and watch over Uncle Mart and Francis." Gene falls asleep protected from the war and the weather in the warmth of his bed.

The 1945 January newspaper headlines renew hope for an early ending to war. Good news is reported nearly every day: "Japanese Air Force Mostly Destroyed in Luzon, Philippines," "American Citizens Liberated in the Philippines," "Soviet Union Army Liberates Warsaw, Poland," "Auschwitz Prisoners Freed by Red Army," "President Roosevelt Sworn in for a Fourth Presidential Term," and "German Army Retreats from the Battle of the Bulge." People are hopeful the war will soon end, and Gene and Jimmy waste little time in celebrating the victories.

Gene, wearing his aviation cap with goggles, and Jimmy in his aviator cap with floppy earflaps reenacts air battles as they go sledding on the snow covered hills near the Hardin Creek. Gene maneuvers his make-believe P-38, and Jimmy flies an imaginary P-51 Mustang attacking Japanese Mitsubishi Zeros. The want-to-be pilots down one Japanese fighter after another. They sometimes dive into a grove of Hackberry trees at the bottom of the snow covered slope. The boys miraculously survive by guiding their sleds into snow drifts under the weathered trees avoiding a plunge into the creek behind the trees.

Sometimes they fall off their sleds, allowing their make believe planes to crash into snow drifts. As they roll across the packed snow, they pretend to have been ejected from their flaming planes and are parachuting to safety. Rising up, they brush themselves off and retrieve their faithful fighter planes from the snow. After they tire of their dogfights, in which they shoot down numerous imaginary Japanese pilots, they head home. They brag to their mothers that once again they've earned the honor of being defenders of the sky, an honor they proudly bestow on themselves. Then they enjoy popcorn as they celebrate their efforts to end the war.

Sometimes Vincent joins them in sledding, using a shovel as his sled. When Gene and Jimmy play war, it's an unwritten code that anyone on a shovel is designated as a Japanese Zero. Vincent holds tightly to the handle of the corn shovel and begins his uncontrolled flight down the hill. From the top of the hill, the two older boys place Vincent in the cross hairs of their machine guns and aim directly at him. In these skirmishes there are a few tears, but never a broken bone, or at least no one ever goes to the hospital for x-rays.

In one dogfight Gene collides with Vincent knocking him off his shovel. Gene claims Vincent is parachuting from his Japanese Zero because his plane is doomed. Regardless of the explanation, Vincent's leg is slashed and Gene can't deny that the red blotch on the snow isn't blood. Worried, the two older boys place Vincent on a sled and pull him to Gene's home. Gene's dad pours Watkins Liniment on the cut, wraps gauze around the injured leg, and awards him a St. Christopher's medal for his bravery. Vincent limps for two weeks but proudly displays the medal on his shirt pocket until school is dismissed for the summer.

With the arrival of spring, a victory is almost assured in Europe. The newspaper explains that President Franklin D. Roosevelt; Prime Minister of England, Winston Churchill; and Secretary General of the Communist Party of the Soviet Union, Joseph Stalin, meet at Yalta. Their purpose is to discuss how Europe will be divided after the defeat of Germany. No one is now talking about "if" the Nazis will be defeated, but only "when" they will be defeated.

Newsreels and newspaper pictures reveal the complete destruction of German cities, showing bombed out cities, bodies in the streets, and starving prisoners released from the prisons and slave camps. There are stories and rumors of Jews in German concentration camps having been gassed to death and burned in cremation plants. The newsreels at the Saturday movies begin to expose a new picture of war, one that is ugly and nauseating.

"Did the Nazis actually burn people in furnaces?" asks Gene.

"We don't know the details, but we do know that thousands of the Jewish people and others who disagreed with the Nazis were placed in prisons and killed," answers his dad.

With the realization that war destroys not only soldiers but also innocent people, warfare no longer seems as glamorous as viewed in the movies or as sterilized as in the censored newsreels. Gene asks, "Will Uncle Mart and Francis be coming home soon?"

"Probably not until the war is over, and about all we can do is to pray for the war to end."

Gene returns home from school on April 12, 1945, and discovers his mom sobbing softly. He doesn't ask any questions but walks outside to see if the violets he is transplanting need watering. He fills a small bucket from the livestock watering tank and pours it on the violets that he has uprooted from the ditch to the garden. His mom comes outside; she is no longer crying but tells Gene, "A special news bulletin from CBS World News reports that President Roosevelt is dead."

"Who will run the country now?" asks Gene.

"Vice-President Truman is now the President. It will be his job to bring an end to this war."

"Was the President killed?" asked Gene.

"No. He has been ill since he was elected President."

"Seems like lots of people are dying," Gene says to himself out loud.

In May the front page of the newspaper features a picture of Mussolini hanging upside down, full of bullet wounds, with Italian partisans standing nearby. The Saturday night movie newsreels reveal pictures of dead bodies piled high alongside a Nazi Prison Camp. The war looks uglier every day, and finally on May 7, 1945, the German forces surrender unconditionally. On May 8th Victory in Europe (V-E Day) is declared. *The Des Moines Register* headlines read: "GERMANY SURRENDERS!"

Reading the headlines, Gene asks his mom again, "Will Uncle Mart and Francis be coming home now?"

"Not for a while," answers his mom.

"When will they come home?"

"Not soon, there is still the war with Japan," his mom replies.

Gene dashes to school earlier than usual the next morning. He enters the school and looks for someone to discuss Germany's surrender but finds the classroom empty. There is a World War II character called Kilroy that appears everywhere the American Army has been. Gene believes Kilroy is needed at Bristol 2 and draws the Kilroy sketch on the blackboard. The doodle is a cartoon-like character peeking over a wall with his bald head and eyes showing and his long nose hooked over the edge of the wall. Kilroy's two hands are drawn on each side of his head as if they are holding him up, so he can peek at whatever or whoever is on the other side. Below he prints, "Kilroy Was Here"

Miss Crowley comes out of the storage room where the coal and cleaning supplies are stored. She approaches smiling at the "Kilroy Was Here" drawing and says, "If Kilroy's here, an American soldier is here somewhere."

Gene laughs, thinking that she must have a boyfriend in the army. If her boyfriend is in the military she is probably happy that Germany has surrendered, but there is no discussion about V - E Day. She rings the school bell and after the students are seated she reminds them, "The war may be over in Europe, but it is still raging in the Pacific. Remember you can still buy saving bond stamps on Friday to help bring an end to the fighting."

In June Gene's mom receives a V-mail letter from her brother PFC Martin Harkins, Uncle Mart. The V-mail letter is microfilmed and printed on a smaller sized sheet of paper. By reducing the size of the letter, the weight of the mail is reduced, speeding up the delivery of mail. His uncle's letter was written on Sunday, May 13, 1945, less than one week after V - E Day. No mention is made of battles or the Nazis' surrender. Military personnel are ordered to reveal no information about the war, and are to restrict to writing only about relatives and family. Letters are censored, and classified information is blacked out. There is nothing blacked out in this May 13, 1945 letter.

PFC Martin Harkins
COH 393INFAPO449
% PM NEW YORK NY
Germany – Sunday - May 13, 1945
Dear Sis and Family
I received your letter and sure was glad to hear from you. I hope this finds every one OK. I am fine. It is sure nice weather here. I sure hope it stays this way. Tell Jerry he will have to learn to whistle if he wants to be like me. I was sorry to hear about Bernard Tiffany, there seems to be a lot of unlucky people. Now days having additions

on the family & I sure would have liked to see Danny catching his rabbits. I bet he had a job. I didn't know LC was sick. I hope it is nothing serious. I thank you for the box now, as it probably will get it in a few days. And I know it will be swell regardless what it is as long as it is from Home. I think I will be able to keep caught up on my writing now so write whenever you can. I got a radio & it sure seems good to listen to music from home after five months of silence. Write soon.
Love Mart.
Relay by V-MAIL

Gene's mother had not heard from her brother for five months. She knows that after an emergency leave in 1944 he was sent to Europe and assigned to the 393rd Infantry Regiment 99th Infantry Division. The 99th is called the Checkerboard Division and nicknamed the Battle Babies because so many inexperienced men were assigned to the division. Nevertheless, it is in part credited for holding the northern Germans' advance at the Battle of the Bulge. Gene's mother also learns that in early March her brother crossed the Ludendorff Bridge only a couple of days after the bridge was captured by the Americans. Gene's godfather is not discharged immediately after VE Day but spends an additional nine months in the Army occupation of Europe. He receives an honorable discharge in 1946 and is awarded the Bronze Star for the various military campaigns in which he was involved. While he continues to visit Iowa and asks to see Gene's head scar, which occurred years earlier, he never talks to Gene about the war.

School is dismissed on May 15, 1945, and as the students leave for summer Miss Crowley tells the students "Don't forget what you've learned." Then she adds, "Let's all wish that the war with Japan is over when we return in August.

Gene reads in the newspaper, and views in the movie newsreels, that there is savage fighting in the Pacific. He hates the Emperor of Japan, Hirohito, and holds him responsible for ordering the deaths of thousands of American sailors, marines, and soldiers. His dad assures Gene that the United States Government is determined to make the emperor surrender unconditionally, and explains that the American Army Air Force has firebombed Tokyo, killing between 100,000 to 200,000 Japanese.

"What is firebombing mean?" asks Gene.

"The bombs start fires that bring massive destruction to the cities, and the fires don't distinguish between soldiers or citizens." His dad go on, "Most Americans don't care. Since the Japanese bombed Pearl Harbor without warning, for no apparent reason; now they must be punished."

A week after school is dismissed, Gene goes to Farlin with his dad to have the mower blade sharpened at the blacksmiths. His dad takes the blade into the blacksmith shop for Charlie to sharpen, and Gene runs over to Mike's Market. Gene searches the wanted posters that are thumb tacked on the bulletin board beside the post office window. Maybe someday he will recognize a real criminal, but his pursuit is interrupted when he hears Mike and Harold Weber talking about the war.

"The Germans had sense enough to give up when they had enough." Harold says about V-D day.

"They were never sneaky, like the Japanese," adds Mike.

"Yeah, we'll teach those Japs what we do when we get sucker punched," states Harold. "Maybe we should just wipe that island off the face of the earth?"

"Let the army take care of Hirohito, Harold. You're a farmer."

"Yeah, I'll stick to something I know about." Harold sees Gene and asks him, "You going to help with the threshing this year young fella?"

"I hope so," answers Gene.

"Harvesting oats is about to begin, and the threshing run is being organized," replies Harold.

Preparing for the harvest begins when the oat fields have turned a golden tan but before they are too dry. Gene's dad uses a horse-drawn McCormick binder, which has been converted, so it can be pulled by his Farmall tractor. The binder cuts oats, ties the straw with twine into bundles, and dumps them in the field. Once the oat bundles are dropped on the field, family members stack the bundles into shocks. The shocks keep the oats off the ground, which permits the wind to blow through the bundles to dry the straw and oats, so they can ripen in preparation for threshing.

The neighborhood farmers who agree to join the threshing run schedule the route and pray for dry weather. The threshing crew consists of neighbors, maybe a hired hand, a water boy, and a large threshing machine that is moved from farm to farm. When the shocks of bundles are completely dry, the threshing run begins.

The bundles of oats are stacked on hayracks. The racks are pulled by horses, and when the racks are full the farmer hauls the load of bundles to the thresher. Two men operate the thresher, which separates the straw from the grain. The straw is blown from the thresher into a large straw stack. The straw is used as livestock bedding during the winter months. The oats are dumped into a wagon while a farmer distributes the oats throughout the wagon. Once the wagon is full, it is pulled by a team of horses to an oat bin usually inside the corn crib; there two men shovel the oats into storage bins. The oats are stored to be used to feed horses and chickens. While one wagon is being emptied of oats, a second wagon is collecting oats at the threshing machine. The men can't afford to waste time, and everyone wants to complete harvesting without being rained on.

This year, Gene and Jimmy both serve as water boys who carry drinking water to the working men. A pony is provided for Jimmy to carry water to the workers in the field. Gene runs ahead of the pony with another jug of water and sometimes catches a ride on a returning hayrack to refill his jug. He is barefoot and learns to run so as not to step directly down on the straw stubbles. If he steps straight down on the stems, it doesn't cut his feet, but it hurts. By the end of summer, his feet are toughened from walking on dirt clods, gravel, and straw stubble.

The neighborhood women aren't left out of the community threshing venture. They cook and feed the crew. They bake pies, cakes, bread and fix huge quantities of potatoes, fried chicken, fresh green beans, peas, and tomatoes. Whenever there is an enormous meal, farmers are often heard to say, "There is enough food here to feed threshers."

And while the farmers are not as orderly as Grant Wood's painting "Dinner for Threshers," it is more fun. When they come in from the field, the men remove the first layer of sweat, straw, dust, and dirt by throwing water on each other from the livestock watering tank, and then they rinse their arms and faces with water from the hand pump. Cleaning up is entwined with horse play: splashing water on each other, grabbing another's straw hat and throwing it in the tank. And once in a while a younger farmhand even ends up in the tank.

The men brag about how hard they work as they sit down at the outdoor table that is made from wooden boards and covered with an array of tablecloths. The dinner talk is filled with stories about finding a bull snake under an oat shock, discovering a fox den near the south fence, and gossiping about who's gambling too much. Once done eating, it's back to work. The men move from farm to farm to thresh the oats, and the women follow them from house to house to prepare the noon meal. The neighborhood is engaged in threshing until all the oats are harvested.

After the threshing run is completed, Gene relaxes playing Cowboy and Indian with his younger brother as a cowboy. They agree that the empty corncrib serves as a safe haven, and if one is in the crib the other can't attack him. Gene uses a meat mallet as his pretend tomahawk and chases his brother across the barnyard as his brother runs for safety in the crib. With a bloodcurdling cry, Gene shakes the mallet. The mallet head flies off the wooden handle, striking his brother in the back of his head and knocking him to the ground. Gene prays his brother's guardian angel is close as blood begins to ooze out of a two-inch long cut. Gene assists the injured cowboy back into the house and pleads, "It's bad, Mom."

His younger brother is rushed to Jefferson to see a doctor and Gene prays again; but this time he includes God, Mary, Joseph, Jesus, the Holy Ghost, and all of the saints. He hopes he hasn't killed his brother, and he knows it's serious since none of the family is ever taken to the doctor's office for stitches. If someone gets cut around the farm, his dad just pours Watkins Liniment over the cut and tapes it shut. While his dad practices his medical skills, the patient is told to stop crying and let it heal. This time the injury is too serious for his dad to patch, and that worries Gene. When they return from the doctor's office, Gene hurries to the car to see how badly the injury is. The cut required ten stitches, giving his brother a lot of attention. There is no punishment for Gene. His parents believe he has learned his lesson and is punishing himself enough by agreeing to take care of his younger brother for a week.

Gene needs a break from the excitement and decides to read *Heidi*, one of the books his teacher loaned him for the summer. He relaxes on the front porch and escapes from Iowa and cowboys and Indians by traveling to the Alps. There he meets Heidi, her grandfather, and Peter. He walks down the mountain and cares for Clara. The story is more interesting than the comics, which he still treasures and keeps in a box under his bed.

Jimmy is more interested in fishing than in reading, and on hot summer afternoons when the corn is heard growing and chickens pant in the shade, Gene joins Jimmy at the Harkin Creek. Before going fishing, Gene digs down about six to eight inches for night crawlers that hide on the north side of the barn. They are easily caught when a spade full of black dirt is overturned. Gene always agrees to bring the worms, and Jimmy is best at assigning them to their death since he can thread a night crawler on a hook quicker than a snapper can blink.

Gene enjoys being outside, but Jimmy loves the outdoors. He can hear wrens caution the dragonflies not to tease the turtles, and he understands the minks chattering when they play on the creek's embankment. Most importantly, he knows when the fish have stopped biting. If he hasn't hooked a bullhead in fifteen minutes, the frogs challenge him to join them in the water. Off comes his jeans, his shirt, and last of all his shorts; he jumps kicking and shouting as he splashes into the muddy water, "Come on in, the water's just right." Gene joins him in skinny dipping and after playing in the creek the two leave as dirty, or dirtier, than when they started playing.

Gene's mom worries when the two venture to the creek. They both know how to swim, but not very well. She fears they might fall from a tree branch when doing their shenanigans to prove they are funnier, riskier, or braver. She encourages them to spend time reading or playing around the farm. But Gene can only read so much and Jimmy doesn't like reading, so they resort to reenacting movies in the farm marsh.

Their favorite movie to perform is the *Fighting Seabees* starring John Wayne and Susan Hayward, and for this movie they invite Vincent's sister Marilyn to be Susan Hayward, which wasn't a very good idea. After the first invitation, Marilyn becomes a real pain by tagging along with Vincent even if there isn't a part for her. They perform the *Fighting Seabees* three times, and both Jimmy and Gene decide that if they join the military service they'll become Seabees, which are members of the Construction Battalion (CB). Their forth reenactment of the movie is done without Vincent or Marilyn.

"We have to beat those dirty Japs" Jimmy shouts as he wades through the ankle-high marsh and holds his fake bolt action Springfield rife above his head. He joins Gene aboard the raft made of discarded lumber. With their weight the raft sinks immediately in the mud and slime. Gene loses his balance and falls into the marsh, covering himself with floating weeds and swamp water.

Laughing, the boys begin pulling the weeds from the bottom of the marsh and placing the swamp plants on the raft. They pretend they are preparing a landing for incoming cargo ships. A Japanese plane appears on the horizon and strafes the small landing craft.

"Bam, Bam, Bam, that was too close," shouts Jimmy as the two throw themselves on the raft to avoid being hit by bullets from the aircraft.

As the enemy plane returns to whatever evil place it calls home, Jimmy says, "I hope they're gone for the day."

"Do you think that is what it is really like?" asks Gene.

"Like what?" replies Jimmy?

"You know, does an enemy plane just shoot at them and then fly away?"

"Maybe. That's how it is in the movies."

"But the newsreels show lots of dead people, and the fighting looks different in the newsreels than in the movies," probes Gene, looking for reasons why the movies and newsreels disagree.

The two forget their task of building a beach landing and discuss the differences between newsreels and movies.

"In the newsreels the dead soldiers are dirty and are missing legs or arms, and in movies when soldiers are killed they always say something before they die and seldom have smashed bodies," comments Gene

He does remembers how much blood he saw when he hit his brother with the pretend tomahawk and when Vincent got cut sledding.

"There must be lots of blood when someone is shot. I'm tired of the war and want it to be over," Gene declares and walks away, leaving Jimmy sitting on the edge of the wooden raft on the far side of the marsh.

The August 6th Gene opens up the *Des Moines Register* and reads, "U. S. Using Atom Bomb!" He reads that the bomb is 2,000 times more powerful than the biggest blockbuster bomb. While destruction details are unavailable because of the dust and smoke over Hiroshima this is one story that says the power of the bomb may have come from the sun's energy. Three days later another atom bomb is dropped on Nagasaki, Japan, and on August 14 *The Des Moines Register* headline boasts: "JAPAN SURRENDERS! TOKYO RADIO REPORTS"

Iowa Governor Blue issues an appeal for a day of thanksgiving and prayer, rather than one of uncontrolled celebration and rowdiness. That morning Gene rides with his dad to Jefferson to pick up a used sofa, and they hear church bells ringing, cars honking, and people dancing and singing on the county court house lawn. World War II is over. It appears that not many people listened to Governor Blue's request to restrain their celebrating.

Gene faithfully reads *The Des Moines Register* and learns that the bomb dropped on August 6, 1945, on the city of Hiroshima, Japan, kills an estimated 80,000 people, and the one dropped on Nagasaki, Japan, kills 70,000 people. Victory over Japan is announced by President Truman on August 14, 1945. On August 15, 1945, Emperor of Japan, Hirohito, announces an unconditional surrender of Japan to the Allied forces. School begins on Monday, August 27, 1945, two weeks after the Japanese surrender. Mrs. Crowley wish came true.

Gene detests every Friday since there is a spelling test. He always learns to spell the ten words from a fifty word spelling list, and is able to use the words in a sentence. The teacher doesn't check to see if he completed his work, but at the end of the week she selects ten words from the week's list and pronounces them to Gene to write correctly on a sheet of paper. He fails the test nearly every Friday. It is unlike him to do poorly in school since most of his grades are A's and B's, but his grades in spelling are erratic and always the poorest of all his subjects. He fails his first six week spelling test, and he expects to do poorly in future tests.

"Gene, you can do better," his mom urges when signing his report card.

"Mom, you know I just can't spell," Gene responds, and the subject is dropped.

Gene can't hear the difference between words like, *well* and *whale*. Nor can he hear a difference between *accept* and *except*, or *sink* and *zinc*. He avoids using words like aluminum, linoleum or purple because others laugh at his pronunciation.

"Miss Crowley, I hear words differently than other students," he tells his teacher.

"Your hearing is good. You just aren't learning your list of spelling words. Work harder," she instructs him.

Mr. Morris, the County Superintendent, visits school and she mentions Gene's difficulty in learning how to spell, and explains this is a contrast to how he does in other subjects.

"Could his spelling problems be related to his hearing?" asks Miss Crowley.

Mr. Morris responds, "I don't believe it is a hearing problem but a cultural one. Gene pronounces words like lots of the people living in this area."

Gene doesn't receive special assistance. There is no speech therapist available, and there is only one county-wide nurse that can be called on when vaccinations are needed or a health inspection is warranted. Gene knows one child in the community who never attends school, and he is told she can't learn. Students with serious educational needs don't attend school. Those with lesser learning difficulties learn to adjust for their problems and some never graduate from the eighth grade and are not admitted into high school.

Gene's hearing problem is slight, and the spelling issue is dropped because his spelling improves. He learns how to compensate for his poor spelling by learning the meanings of words even if he can't spell or pronounce them, and finds substitutes for the words when he writes. If he can't spell *enlightenment* but knows it means to make brighter, he uses the words: *make brighter* or *to glow*. He memorizes words from sight, without sounding them out, because he doesn't hear all of the sounds. He overcomes his poor spelling, and by the second semester his spelling grades jump from D's to A's. He continues to receive A's through the eighth grade. However, his choice of words in writing assignments is sometime humorous and sometimes confusing. The root for his poor spelling may be his family pronunciation, his hearing, or a combination of both; but neither hearing nor speech specialists are available at Bristol 2.

Where Did All the Cowboys Go?

There are no immediate changes at Bristol 2 following the surrender of the Japanese, but some changes are noticeable in the community. At the 1945 family Christmas dinner Gene's relatives are visiting about some of the changes.

Gene's mom believes it's unfair that a neighbor woman is required to leave her job working at a manufacturing company.

"Remember she signed a contract agreeing that at the end of war she would leave her job once the men returned from the military," one of the aunts replies.

"Yes, but now she is searching for a teaching job. It's a good thing she was a teacher before she went to work at the factory."

"There will be lots of changes in 1946," replies his Aunt Leona.

Gene goes into the dining room where the men are drinking a cup of coffee.

As he puts on his coat to join his cousins who are playing outside, Gene hears his dad and his uncles talking.

"How soon will cars be available for everyone?" ask Gene's Uncle Taylor.

"Who knows?" replies Uncle Frank.

"I'm more interested in buying some new farm machinery, my equipment is pretty much worn out," answers Gene's dad.

They continue their dreaming about having better times and hoping that the rationing will end. Gene doesn't remember what it was like before the war, but he is interested in tasting bananas, chewing bubble gum, and seeing his cousin and Godfather return from Europe.

Gene stops before opening the door and asks, "When do you think the soldiers are returning?"

"It will be awhile, and Francis and Mart probably won't be here until sometime next year" answers his Uncle Frank. "But we can be thankful the fighting has stopped."

Part Two 1946 to 1950

Nearly four years of war leaves the American people eager to forget the losses resulting from the global conflict. Some wish to return to the prewar days, but there is no choice except to go forward. For those who remember little prior to 1941, the past is of little consequence. Those who fought the war, both at home and overseas, are prepared to protect the youth physically and socially, and create a prosperous nation. Using lessons learned and technology discovered the leaders begin to forge a new path for United States, and from 1946 until 1950 the foundation for what they hope will become Camelot begins to unfold.

Gene and Jimmy return from an unsuccessful fishing excursion.

1946

Overnight, strong winds created snowdrifts, burying clusters of cornstalks and dead branches. All night long, the on-again off-again blizzard cut and chiseled the mountains of snow leaving a shrine to the storm. Now a gentle breeze engraves the final touches on the white marble monuments. And while the invisible artist etches the final touches in memory of the storm, it is chilling to realize the darkness that is beneath the picturesque memorials.

The snowstorm has held Gene and his family captive for nearly four days, and he hasn't left the house except when he accompanies his dad to do chores. Gene now needs to escape the closeness of the indoors and enjoy the mixture of snow, sunshine, and fresh air. He wants to explore what is beneath the huge mounds of snow.

He removes his coat from a hook behind the kitchen door and informs anyone who is listening, "I'm going outside to climb the drifts."

"I'd rather you wait until the wind dies down completely," replies his mom and then adds, "How about a game of Chinese Checkers?"

She removes six bags of marbles and asks, "Which color marbles do you want?"

"I'll take white," Gene replies as he returns his coat to the hook.

"Anyone else to join us?" his mom asks as she arranges the game on the dining room table. His dad is sitting in a cloth upholstered chair and alternates between snoozing and reading about Yellowstone National

Park from an Encyclopedia. His younger brother, stretched out on the floor, builds a log house using Lincoln Logs, a gift he received for Christmas. His older brothers are busy; one is sitting on the living room sofa reading *Hans Brinker,* the other listening to *Boston Blackie* on the radio. Gene and his mother, hearing no takers, begin the game.

Gene starts by moving one marble from his triangle toward his mother's triangle on the opposite side of the hexagon. The goal is to move the marbles, which Gene pretends are soldiers, to his mother's triangle by jumping marbles or moving them one space at a time. At the same time his mother takes turns moving her marbles toward Gene's triangle. Whoever gets all of their marbles placed in the opponent's triangle first is the winner. It is not a war game or very aggressive, but a rather simple game that involves competition and winning -- both of which his mother enjoys.

A continuous ring of the telephone interrupts the game and commands the attention of the snow-bound family; a nonstop ring means there is a public announcement from the central telephone office. Gene's mom listens to the message.

"What's that about?" Gene's dad asks.

His mother informs the family, "It was Clara at the telephone office. The storm has ended, and all county roads will be open by tomorrow morning. It is back to normal, and that means back to school for you guys."

Since the end of the war, the newspaper is reporting more and more about the crimes committed by Nazis and Japanese military. Gene's interest is heightened by the photographs of dead bodies stacked outside prison camps, newsreels of starving women and children, and haunting pictures of men wearing only rags and skin. There is no life behind their sunken eyes, and there is no doubt that Jews, political prisoners, Gypsies, and those who fought the Nazis were victims of hatred.

In the classroom Miss Crowley remarks, "The dark side of human behavior imprisoned the Nazis' souls and they are guilty of cruel and cold-blooded treatment of other humans."

Gene replies, "My dad says that the Nazis hate the Jews and that hate only nurtures evil."

"Will the Nazis be punished for their crimes?" asks Jimmy.

"Yes," responds Miss Crowley. They are being put on trial at Nuremberg, Germany."

"Why not just kill the Nazis?" asks Gene. He believes the United States Army should imprison or execute them – no need for trials.

"The United States generals and all of the Allies believe the world should see these men, and let everyone know what they did," answers Miss Crowley. "The free world must prove to all people that justice will be done."

"What about the Japs?" Gene asks. "I heard that they even ate some of their prisoners, and made lampshades from the skins of Marines."

"They are called Japanese, not Japs," his teacher corrects him. "And those responsible for war crimes will be tried at the Tokyo War Crimes Trials."

"If other tyrants see that evil governments and military dictators are held responsible maybe wars will end," adds Miss Crowley.

In the newspaper Gene reads, many stories depicting the Nuremburg War Trials, but only a few about Tokyo War Crimes Trials. The Nuremburg War Trials start in November, 1945 and end in October, 1946. The Tokyo War Crimes Trials start April, 1946 and end in November, 1948. No one can explain to Gene why the newspaper prints more stories about the Nuremburg Trials. His dad argues that people are tired of hearing about the killing and hating. Without doubt, the American people want to forget the war, and returning soldiers are reluctant to talk about it.

Soldiers coming home are returning to work, and many are taking advantage of the GI Bill, which provides an opportunity to receive a college education. Ration stamps are becoming a thing of the past, except sugar which is rationed until June, 1946. England, unlike the USA, continues to ration several items including tea and sugar until 1953. Recovery will take longer in England because of the massive destruction done by German bombing raids.

Changes are coming quickly to the United States, and life is attempting to pick up where it left off prior to the war. The Rural Electrification Administration (REA) is one such example. The Roosevelt Administration started the program in 1935 to bring electricity to rural America. It slowed down and finally quit during the war, but it is now back on track and will create a huge transformation to those who do not have electricity.

Up and down the gravel road, trucks haul creosote utility poles and create clouds of dust. Workmen dump the poles into the ditches, crushing the wild strawberries and wild roses that are scattered along the roadside. Their racket is followed by the commotion of men who operate an earth auger that is digging large postholes. When the holes are dug, a crane operator sets the poles. Two ground workers assist the crane operator as they straighten and pack dirt around the poles. Linemen scamper up and down the utility poles attaching the electrical wire to insulators. Electricity is eventually coming to all of Bristol Township in Greene County, Iowa.

"Dad, will we have electricity tonight?" Gene calls from the roof of the chicken coop where he has been watching the work crews.

"Probably not tonight, but we will by the end of summer," he answers and then jokes, "No need for Aladdin lamps this winter."

Gene's dad and his cousin Francis, who has returned from the war, have wired the house in anticipation of electricity, but wiring the barn will wait for another year. They mount light fixtures on the walls of the three bedrooms and place a single ceiling light fixture in the kitchen, living room, and dining room. They place one electrical outlet in every room except the kitchen; there they place three outlets in anticipation of future kitchen appliances and a special outlet for an electric range. There is no light fixture in the attached unheated washroom, only a single bulb that hangs from the ceiling, and the outdoor toilet is not wired. The kerosene lantern that is used to make night visits will remain in the washroom.

In a moment of enthusiasm, Gene's dad purchases a second-handed Hot Point Range and surprises Gene's mom by bringing it home. Fearing that he might equip the entire kitchen without her, she quickly purchases a new Sub-Zero deep freezer and has it delivered immediately. She then places her name on waiting lists for a new Sears Cold Spot refrigerator and a new electric Maytag washing machine. For the next two months, the family steps carefully around the range and freezer, waiting for the arrival of the refrigerator and washing machine.

By the summer of 1946, the magic of electricity has arrived, and the four major appliances are installed. The old appliances are stored in the coal shed.

"Flip the switch and the lights are on," shouts Gene's five year old brother as the boy repeatedly turns the dining room lights on and off.

"Flip it off and leave it off. Electricity isn't free," lectures their mom.

Electricity isn't the only first that Gene experiences in 1946. There is bubble gum.

"Try this piece of Super Bubble Gum. Just chew it and blow a bubble; chew it again, blow another bubble," Jimmy tells Gene.

"Does it lose its flavor?" asks Gene.

"The fun isn't in the flavor but in seeing how big you can blow a bubble."

The two compete in a dual bubble blowing contest, seeing who can blow the biggest bubble.

"We even bought some bananas at the grocery store last week" Gene brags to Jimmy.

"We got there too late; all of the bananas were gone. What'd they taste like?"

"Okay."

"Well, were they sweet or sour?" asks Jimmy.

"Sweet," Gene replies, limiting additional information from his friend as he blows an extra large bubble.

"Wow that was some bubble."

"Bananas are fine, kind of mushy, and Mom thinks they are too expensive. I like bubble gum better," replies Gene.

"How about fishing next week after the school picnic? School will be out, and the crappie are still biting," Jimmy encourages Gene.

"Can't. My younger brother, Mom, and I are catching a train at Farlin. We're going to Des Moines," Gene boasts.

"You lucky dog," Jimmy replies as he starts walking home.

Two days later Gene, his younger brother, and his mom board a train in Farlin to visit his Aunt Veronica and Uncle Arnold in Des Moines, Iowa. Once on the train, they are escorted to a passengers' coach where several soldiers, salesmen, and businessmen are seated. Additional passengers come on board the train at Jefferson and Perry. The sun has set by the time the train arrives in Des Moines, and Gene is stunned by the city's night lights. On the farm the dark night sky is crowded with stars; here in the city the night sky seems empty of stars. Stars are hidden by the bright city lights, but they reappear in the sky around Drake University.

His aunt has several events for Gene to enjoy in Des Moines. He experiences the boat rides at the Old Dutch Mill located on the Iowa State Fair Grounds, rides a city bus, and splashes in a wading pool near Drake University. Riding the bus to the wading pool, he learns more than the bus schedule. Boarding the bus, Gene hurries to the rear and begins bouncing on the seat that extends across the bus.

"Come up here in front," orders his cousin.

"I like it back here, the seat is really bouncy," replies Gene.

"Well, you can't sit back there, so come up here now," his cousin repeats.

Gene reluctantly complies and joins his cousin in a seat near the front of the bus. At the next bus stop, several boys with dark colored skin board the bus, walk to the rear, and get comfortable on the large seat. These boys, plus Gene and his cousin, leave the bus at the same time and head for the wading pool. Gene joins them playing around the large spray of water in the center of the pool.

Several white children shout, "Get over here."

Deflated, Gene retreats from the spray and joins his cousin sitting on the edge of the pool.

On the return bus trip Gene remembers not to sit in the rear of the bus, and his cousin tells him, "They are colored people and you are not to sit in the back of the bus or play with them at the pool."

Gene naively responds, "Why do they get to have all the fun?"

Gene had seen African people in books and movies before his trip to Des Moines. He enjoys the *Tarzan* movies, where Africans are shown as savages. He examines the school's *National Geographic* magazines and reads articles about gorillas, spotted leopards, and sometimes peeks at pictures of the black naked women. His trip to Des Moines is the first time he actually sees colored people, and he doesn't understand why he can't play with them.

He has never thought much about a person's skin color. His skin is white with freckles. His mother skin is very fair, and Charlie, the blacksmith, is brown but not African. Pat, a neighboring farmer, is a big Irishman with pink cheeks. When Gene is told that he is white, he replies, "Not really, I'm spotted."

Nor has he really listened to how people talk; everyone in his neighborhood sounds the same. He and his father listen to *Amos n Andy* on the radio, but the two men are not real black people. His dad tells him that the two men talking and telling jokes are actually white men.

After returning from Des Moines, he participates in an activity which shows black people differently than the *Tarzan* movies, the *National Geographic*, or the *Amos n Andy* radio program. It's a black-face minstrel show in Farlin.

"Don't burn the cork too much; we don't want ash," instructs Mr. Allen, who is in charge of the performance.

"Smear the burnt cork on his face real good and be sure not to miss his ears, we don't want a black man with white ears," laughs the overweight director.

"Do I have to wear red lipstick?" asks Gene.

"We want the audience to see your lips move when you sing. Get out there, have fun, and sing your heart out. And don't forget to do a little dancing; Negroes are good at dancing."

Gene walks onto the stage of the IOOF Hall in Farlin and starts singing.

> I come from Alabama with my banjo on my knee,
> I'm going to Louisiana, my true love for to see
> It rained all night the day I left, the weather it was dry
> The sun so hot I froze to death: Susana, don't you cry.
> Oh! Susanna Oh! Don't you cry for me
> I've come from Alabama
> With my banjo on my knee.

There are about thirty adults and ten children in the audience, and the stuffy IOOF Hall hasn't cooled off from the August afternoon. At the end of Gene's performance, they stamp their feet and applaud wildly, more as if they are participants in the act than actually enjoying the program.

Gene bows and hurries off the stage to remove the lipstick and brunt cork from his face. His performance is followed by several boys in black face, who tell some jokes. Then a high school boy sings two more songs: "Old Black Joe" and "Swanee River." When the show ends, cookies, iced tea, and lemonade are served. The men go outside into the evening air and light up cigarettes; a few fill their pipes and fumble with matches to light them. They talk about crops.

Gene, other members of the cast, and children from the audience grab some cookies and lemonade and find a corner in the old hall to talk about school, which starts next week.

Near the front of the building, Gene's mother is engaged in a heated discussion with Mrs. Allen. Gene isn't close enough to hear everything, but he hears enough to know his mom isn't pleased about the show. She didn't want to attend, but she wanted to hear Gene sing.

"That's right, I didn't like it. I don't like blackface minstrel shows," his mom is saying.

"You listen to *Amos n Andy* on the radio don't you, and what about Al Jolson? He is one of the best singers alive, and his trademark is his black face. What's different about the minstrel shows?" ask Mrs. Allen.

"Al Jolson isn't singing anymore, Mary. And minstrel shows seem wrong, like we're making fun of the Negroes. We shouldn't be making fun of people."

Gene can't hear Mrs. Allen's reply, so he edges a little closer. Then he hears her remark, "I know Negroes is people, but they ain't the same as us."

"Singing some Stephen Foster songs doesn't seem all that wrong," interrupts a third woman whom Gene doesn't know.

"It isn't just singing songs or even the jokes, but it's making black people seem stupid so others laugh at them," Gene's mother comments.

She then says, "When my grandparents came to the United States the Irish were discriminated against. People didn't hire them because they were Irish; people made fun of them and called them Micks. They said the Irish had hot tempers and liked to fight and that they prayed to the Pope."

His mother is becoming more annoyed as she continues. "We just fought a war to keep hatred out of this country. Let's not forget it."

The women are quiet, and then his mother says firmly, "I don't want my sons to grow up disliking someone just because they attend another church or are of a different color."

No one replies, and she adds as if making the final statement in a court argument, "Colored people have the same feelings that we do, and Al Jolson isn't as popular as he once was. Times change, and people must change with the times."

This is the only minstrel show that Gene performs in.

Gene believes he is too old to play cowboys and Indians, but he does remind Jimmy that Gene Autry is out of the US Air Force and is singing again.

"Gene Autry's "Sioux City Sue" is a big hit," Gene tells Jimmy.

"I don't care. That's kid's stuff," responds Jimmy.

Nor are the two interested in mock battles with the Japanese Imperial Army or the Nazis' Armed Forces. Hirohito is forced to step down as the divine ruler of Japan but remains Emperor of Japan because he helps negotiate an end of fighting with Japan. And Hitler committed suicide when the Russians invaded Berlin. The Allies have won the war, so there is no need for the boys to reenact the battles. Furthermore, they have no place to fight the battles.

The soggy marsh where the boys waged war and fought many brave battles is drained. Tiling crews have dug a trench and laid clay tile that carries the standing water underground to the nearest stream. Numerous ponds and marshes disappear from the Greene County landscape.

Once summer arrives, Gene misses floating on his homemade raft during the rainy season and wading in the tall marsh grass searching for snakes and turtles. The marsh has provided a wonderful backdrop for him to expand his imagination and increase his interest in outdoors and science. Now the marshy area is replaced by straight rows of corn that continue for half a mile before being stopped by a fence. And it appears that nothing will save the cattails, milkweeds, and the occasional muskrat lodge from fading into Iowa's history like the American Indians.

There is no encouragement to keep the wetlands, and farmers are praised for controlling the environment. The information seems counter to what Gene had learned about the Indians from his dad.

"Our teacher thinks getting rid of the marshes is a good idea and that farmers should control their environment. She says that American Indians were primitive people who had no control over the land. Do you think that's true?" Gene asks his dad.

"We drain the wetlands, so we can farm more land and raise more crops," answers his dad. "And maybe draining the marshes is a sign of civilization or maybe it is a sign of greed. The one thing I do know is that you can't stop change even if it isn't progress."

"I guess so?" questions Gene. "But maybe someday we'll want some of those marshes back."

"Don't be glum, you're worrying again. You can't do one thing about it," answers his dad. "Concentrate on the reading contest that is coming up next week as that is something you can do something about."

Earlier in the year the County School Superintendent delivered several reading selections to the teachers in rural schools. There were three stories for the lower grades and another three for the upper grades. Gene is selected to read in the upper level contest but doesn't know which selection he will be asked to read. Therefore, Miss Crowley encourages him to practice reading all of the selections. He takes them home and reads them, rereads them, and practices them until he is soon performing rather than reading.

When the contest date arrives, his dad takes him to Farlin for the Bristol Township Reading Contest. His dad then goes on to Jefferson to conduct some business and instructs Gene to wait at Mrs. Bauman's home until he comes back through Farlin.

Gene doesn't read the selection; he performs it and finishes first in the upper grade level reading contest for Bristol. This is his introduction to competition on the stage, and he enjoys it. And while the competition is as much a contest among the teachers as it is for the students, Gene is a willing partner and learns that he likes being on the stage and the experience of winning.

After the contest, he walks across the road with Mrs. Bauman, an elderly woman who writes local stories for the Greene County newspapers. She is a long-time resident of Farlin and attends the reading contests every year. She was born in a log cabin in Illinois in the late 1800s and moved to Iowa in 1918 with her husband. At her home she always has something for him to eat and lots of house plants to admire.

"You read very well, Gene," she tells him.

"Thanks, I like reading," he answers as they enter her small, neat home. He is met by the fresh smell of drying laundry and fresh cookies baked earlier in the day. The window sills are lined with African violets, begonias, ivy, Mother-in-laws Tongue, and Aloe Vera plants. Gene likes to look at the plants and asks questions about them.

"The fluid from this one," as she points to the Aloe Vera, "is used to ease pain and heal burns. And this begonia can be set outside once spring arrives."

"You know as much about house plants as my dad does about cattails, milkweeds, and bull thistles," Gene compliments her.

She replies, "When I came to Iowa years ago from Indiana, there were countless cattails around the many marshes that dotted Bristol Township."

"I miss the marsh on our farm."

"Me too," the longtime resident repeats, "Me too."

———

Gene's interest in imaginary games is being replaced by group activities. One organization that is available to the farm boys are the 4-H clubs found in all of the Greene County townships. Members learn about farming, responsibility, and leadership. There are also girl 4-H clubs in each township that teach leadership and responsibility to young women. Girls concentrate on cooking, baking, and sewing. The boy and girl club members gather for box socials, hayrides, and dances. Membership is open to all boys and girls who are ten years old or above, and Gene is eager to join his two older brothers who belong to the Bristol Hawkeyes 4-H club.

"How about joining the Bristol Hawkeye's 4-H club?" asks Gene's dad.

"When can I attend the first meeting?" He is excited to meet new friends and participate in the social and sports activities as much as learn about farming.

"We will attend the April meeting with your older brothers and talk to Mr. Lenders. I'm sure he'll sign you up as a member. You turned ten on Sunday April 6 and the meeting is Tuesday."

Members are expected to raise an animal or animals, to build furniture, or plant a garden as a project. The purpose is to teach responsibility as much as to learn a skill. For those who raise animals, it isn't considered a pet but an economic venture, and they are expected to keep records of expenses and profits. At the end of the county fair, the animal is often sold, and it is recorded as to how much money was earned or lost. The record book also provides a year's history of the member's involvement in 4-H activities.

On Tuesday Gene rides to the Farlin with his brothers and dad to attend the meeting in the IOOF Hall.

"You must be Gene?" asks Mr. Lenders.

"Yes."

"And how old are you?"

"I was ten Sunday,"

"You're old enough. Sit down in the first row of chairs, and we will sign you up at the beginning of the meeting," directs the balding farmer who lives east of town.

All members rise and stand, placing their right hand over their heart. The club president leads the 4-H pledge.

> I pledge my Head to clearer thinking,
> my Heart to greater loyalty,

my Hands to larger service,

my Health to better living,

for my club, my community and my country.

Gene is introduced as a new member and is given information about 4-H, a card with the pledge typed on it, and an information sheet with questions for him to complete and return at next month's meeting.

The registration form requests his name, address, and information about his project. He hasn't thought about a project. Meanwhile a man from the county extension office is addressing the meeting.

"If you plan to exhibit your animal at the Greene County Fair, you'll need to complete the entry forms and return them to the county office by July 15th. And remember our motto is to make the best better."

Riding home with his Dad and brothers, Gene asks. "What is a good project; one that will win a blue ribbon?"

"I want to sell my rabbits. You can buy a pair and have rabbits as your project," his oldest brother replies.

"Sounds good," his dad advises.

"And you can start right away," answers his brother.

"Be careful or you'll have too many rabbits by fair time; you have to know how to control their natural desires," advises his dad. Both his dad and brother laugh.

"That can't be too hard," answers Gene. "I just start with two rabbits, and they have a family and I've got everything under control."

"It's not that simple. Can you even tell the difference between the male and female?" asks his brother. Are you sure you want rabbits as your project?"

"Yeah," replies Gene.

"Okay, we start Saturday."

Saturday morning Gene and his brother go to the rabbit cages, and his brother teaches him how to differentiate between the female and male by feeling for their genitalia. He explains that rabbits breed very easily and that just having a bunch of bunnies isn't the rabbit business.

Someone raising rabbits needs to decide when the doe is going to give birth to the bunnies.

Gene's older brother explained to him there are three basic ways to make money in raising rabbits: they can be raised for their fur, or for their meat, or they can be sold as Easter Bunnies. Easter Bunnies are cute and it is easy money, but the practice is discouraged because most of the furry little guys die when separated too early from their mothers. Selling rabbits for their fur requires selling them to companies that can sell the fur to clothing companies. Marketing rabbits to grocery stores or individuals for their meat is the most practical, and the fall is the best time, but the bunnies must be at least two months old before they are sold.

In May Gene buys two of the rabbits and the rest are sold to a local butcher in Jefferson. Gene purchases a buck and a doe with money loaned to him from his dad. The following week Gene places the buck in the doe's pen; the doe is impregnated, and after waiting twenty-five days she makes her nest inside the rabbit hutch. Three days later, six bunnies, each about the size of Gene's thumb, are born with no hair and eyes closed. In two weeks they are covered with fur, their eyes open, and they leave the nest to join the mother in the outside pen. In twenty-five days the mother weans them, and the male and female bunnies are separated.

At the July 4-H meeting, Gene completes the fair entry forms entering his New Zealand white market rabbit as a fair entry in the Greene County Fair. He and his brother select one of the better does with thick snowy white fur, pink eyes, healthy delicate ears, and clean teeth to exhibit at the fair. The rabbit receives a blue ribbon. In the first year, Gene's first 4-H project taught him about marketing, responsibility, dependability, and something not included in the 4-H packet – sex. He is raising rabbits and receives his first blue ribbon.

―――

Gene starts the fifth grade in September 1946 with a brand new teacher he soon calls Miss No Mistakes. She is a recent college graduate and has little experience in teaching. Gene's past behavior in school has generally met the teacher's expectations, and his deportment grades are all A's, B's. The evaluations of his citizenship traits and conduct have always been "Trait Well Developed." And the incidents with Henry at his old school and the pushing and shoving in the cloak room with his buddy Jimmy are typical. Gene's not perfect, but he does behave, maybe because he doesn't want to invite punishment from his mother. But Gene is also easy to control – just keep him busy.

Clichés that Gene hears at family dinners help explain his behavior. "Busy hands are happy hands," "You can lead a horse to water, but you can't make him drink," and "You attract more bees with honey than vinegar." While these sayings don't sum up his behavioral patterns, they do provide an outline for teaching him. Gene likes to be busy, doesn't like being forced, and responds favorably when praised for a job well done.

Every teacher does not get along with every student, and every student does not get along with every teacher. Both, teacher and student, must learn to adjust to the other in order to be successful. This new teacher doesn't use the carrot approach to encourage performance. To her credit, she immediately establishes expectations for all students. Gene is slow in accepting her expectations, and his grades drop from A's to B's and C's. More of a concern to his parents is that his deportment grades drop from A's to C-. His ratings for carefulness, courtesy, fairness, and industry -- which are considered essential to good citizenship -- are reduced to needing improvement. Gene can do better.

The teacher faithfully follows the textbook and state curriculum guides. Gene would rather draw a graph of how much corn is grown by various states or create a map of where major dams exist than to write a report. Miss No Mistakes wants both, a written report and the drawings. She requires that the student's name be written in the upper right hand corner of the paper and warns students if they do not write their name on a worksheet, the grade will be reduced. Erasing spelling words and arithmetic answers is something Gene does regularly, and he has become accustomed to using his eraser.

Gene begins to dislike school, and before long he dislikes studying and finds ways to act out – resulting in even lower citizenship marks.

"Gene, you can do better," his teacher insists.

"I'm working as hard as I can," Gene answers.

"Well, you aren't careful as your papers are messy and full of erasure marks."

"I'll try to do better," Gene halfheartedly responds.

The next day there is a repeat conversation.

"Gene you don't exert enough effort."

"I know."

"Gene, you aren't respecting other students who are working hard at their studies."

"I promise to do better."

Every week there are similar exchanges, and by December the discussions change. He begins losing self-confidence.

"Gene, I want to discuss your arithmetic work," his teacher says, directing Gene to come to her desk.

"I know I'm not very neat," he says as he approaches her desk. "And I don't always hand my assignments in on time. I guess I just don't try hard enough. I'm not very smart."

He completes his fifth grade with an overall average of B-. His deportment is a C-. And his parents are told that he needs to improve in carefulness, courtesy, dependability, fairness, and industry. They aren't critical of the teacher, but Gene's grades are not what his parents want to see and they continue to urge him to improve.

Gene's bag of marbles is becoming smaller and smaller, as he loses when playing "Losers Weepers, Winners Keepers" at school, a game where students place glass marbles inside a circle that is drawn in the dirt. Students take turns and attempt to knock the other person's marbles out of the circle using a larger marble. Marbles knocked out of the ring belong to the person who knocked them out.

"If you're losing, why do you play?" asks his mother.

"I think I'll win more back the next game."

"Are you being taken advantage of?"

"I don't know?"

"Well, if you know someone is cheating to win, it's your own fault," she lectures. "Let them know that you know they are swindling you and stop playing."

"I know, don't let people take advantage of you," is Gene's answer.

"Yes, there are times you must stand up for your rights," his mother responds.

Gene's mom and dad do not believe fighting is a way to resolve problems, but they do believe that there are times a boy must defend himself. So when his Uncle Frank gave the boys boxing gloves for Christmas, they approved. Gene's Grandpa Harkin and his Uncle Frank still argue about James Braddock's win over Max Baer in 1935. But for them it was more than just a boxing match it was a conflict between the Irish and the Germans.

Gene doesn't like boxing when they practice. Both of his older brothers are quicker, larger, and more skilled. When they spar with him, he avoids being hit and keeps out of their reach. And he isn't interested in the 4-H boxing matches that are being scheduled at Farlin's IOOF Hall. However, being poorly prepared doesn't keep him from being paired to fight another boy. All of the 4-H boys are expected to participate in the summer boxing event.

On the night of the boxing event, the air is stale in the old building, and the muggy evening summer air seeps in and encircles the folding chairs, which are assembled around the boxing ring. Gene is paired to fight a boy his age, and he enters the ring with mixed feelings. He wants to do what is expected of him and to look good, but he doesn't want to hurt the other boy nor be hurt. He forgets the number one rule when you box: your goal is to hurt the other person.

The referee strikes his jack knife against a school bell in the stuffy hall to begin the match. Gene and his opponent leave their corners, wearing no head protection or mouth guards. The good thing is that neither wants to hurt the other. But the crowd wants a fight.

"Hit him in the stomach," shouts Mike the owner of Mike's Market Store.

"Smack him, Gene!" shouts another adult. "Mix it up."

Gene turns to see who is doing the shouting and feels the pain on the right side of his face. It is a direct hit to his ear. Tears leak from his right eye. *I'm not going to cry… I'm not going to cry… I'm not going to cry,* he repeats to himself.

Gene doesn't remember exactly what happens, but he rushes toward the other boy swinging both gloves. There is no reason for his fury. He just wants to get even and stop any tears that might be coming.

The crowd cheers the unruly behavior.

Gene hits his opponent several times, and the boy bends over holding his stomach. The referee rings the bell. The second and third rounds are calmer. The adults in the crowd encourage the boys to fight, but the boys have been hurt enough not to inflict any more pain on each other. They chase each other around the ring and pretend to swing powerful punches, hoping they miss their marks.

The referee sounds the bell ending the match and calls the fight a draw. The two boys remove their gloves, shake hands, and leave the ring so another fight can begin. After the fight Gene and his opponent talk about how good the other is at boxing and then drop the subject.

The parish priest must have heard about the boxing matches and schedules some boxing exercises after Saturday catechism. Or maybe he watched the *Bells of St Mary's* or *Going My Way* one too many times and thinks he is Bing Crosby. To justify the matches, he tells the boys that boxing keeps their minds off girls. Gene dislikes the idea of boxing again. Fighting might be okay in solving a dispute with his brothers or in resolving a disagreement on the playground, but to put on gloves and hit another boy who has done nothing to him makes no sense.

The priest matches Gene with an older boy since Gene is taller than most of the boys in his grade. Gene, remembering the sting and ringing in his ear from his early experience, relies on his defensive style of boxing. He throws a few fake punches, protects his face, and dances around. Gene's fighting skills aren't what the priest had hoped for, and when Gene leaves the ring the priest whispers, "You're a disappointment. Your attitude doesn't match your reddish hair. Where is the Irish temper?"

Gene doesn't like to fight, but he does enjoy doing things in which he doesn't know what the result might be, like the time he mixed large red ants around a hill of smaller black ants that resulted in an ant war. Or the time he tosses a TNT firecracker into the cattle tank of water to see what might happen. The explosion beneath the surface of the water blew the rivets out that were holding the tank together. Water immediately spurted out the seams of the metal tank empting the tank of its contents. His experiments are not always exciting, but they are interesting like discovering ways to preserve carrots for rabbits.

Before Thanksgiving 1946, when the ground is unfrozen, Gene digs a hole behind the barn. He lines it with straw, places a five gallon pail in the hole, and fills it with layers of carrots and dried clover. He places an old rug over the pail and adds more straw on top of the old rug. He then heaps dirt over the buried carrots, creating a slight mound, and covers it with more straw and caps it with a feed sack weighted down with four large rocks. With the carrots placed in storage, he waits for the ground to freeze.

Christmas vacation begins on Friday, December 20, and there have been several hard freezes and some light snow. On Saturday, his curiosity is too much. He uncovers the buried clover and carrots and finds them in excellent condition. He removes a handful of clover and seven carrots to feed his rabbits an early Christmas meal. He replaces the rug, the straw, and the sacks over the hidden stash of rabbit food.

Entering the kitchen, he shouts, "Mom, my experiment worked. The clover and carrots stayed dry and fresh."

"That's good. You're here just in time to help string the new electric lights on the Christmas tree," replies his mother. Usually the tree is fully decorated a week before Christmas, but this year his mother wants to be sure the tree isn't too dry. The *Jefferson Bee,* a local newspaper, printed several articles warning about the danger of electric lights and dry evergreen trees. Gene removes the string of lights from the box and hands them to his mom as she places them on the tree.

His mother plugs in the new string of lights. "How do they look?" she asks.

"Good, really good," comments Gene. "This is going to be a good Christmas."

"You have until January 6 to relax."

"And I'm going to enjoy it; all I need to do is feed my rabbits and do chores."

"Don't forget you will need to help your dad clean the barn on Saturday."

"Yeah, but there is still plenty of time to go sledding with Jimmy, and maybe I'll get a book for Christmas. I'll have plenty to do: either reading inside or playing outside."

1947

There is little snow over Christmas vacation, so Jimmy and Gene don't go sledding. Two books, *Who Took the Papers* and *Andy Lane – Fifteen Days in the Air,* are received as gifts and Gene reads both books the first week. During the second week, he bugs his younger brother either asking him to play in the hayloft or asking him to help with chores. And nearly every night he pops popcorn and mixes it with freshly made chocolate candy, which he shares with the family. The popcorn ritual and annoying his younger brother are getting on his mother's nerves, and after the two week vacation she is happy to see school begin.

Pleasing Miss No Mistakes is not what Gene is looking forward to, but he is eager to plot mischievous schemes with Jimmy and Vincent to lessen the boredom of school. Jimmy claims that memorizing the names of state capitals, the multiplication tables, and endless lists of spelling words will destroy a person's brain cells. Last October he even faked phony headaches for overworking his brain. The teacher caught on but never did discover that he was faking his ability to predict oncoming snow storms, a skill that earned the students an early release twice in December. Vincent joined in by lying that he had a week end full of church activities at Thanksgiving, and Miss No Mistakes excused him from doing his homework.

Gene's mother, fearing that he will get into trouble with the teacher, offers him advice as he leaves for school. "Don't be difficult. Complete your assignments on time and do the best you can."

"I will," is his lone response as he steps outside onto the fresh snow that has fallen overnight. He arrives at school to discover that the four-inch blanket of snow has hidden the playground scars left by rambunctious students. Thinking about his mom's advice he asks himself, *how can I keep out of trouble?* The snow covered playground provides him his answer: it's a perfect landscape and an ideal day to play the first game of "Fox and Geese."

He is a master engineer, or so he thinks, for designing the circular patterns needed for playing the game. The rabbits have not tracked across the grounds, and because of Gene's early arrival the field is untouched by students. He starts by stomping out a large circular path around the perimeter of the playground. He then cuts the large circle in half by walking in a straight line from one side to the other. He makes another path across the circle and repeats the pattern until there are three paths across the snow, creating six pie-shaped pieces. The circle is large enough for him to create an inside circle halfway between the center of the circle and the outer rim. Finished, he stands back to admire his work: there is a large outer loop that encircles the playground, spokes connecting the rim to the center, and the extra touch – a middle circle. From the sky it must appear as a large "bulls-eye" carved into the snow. The center of the circle, where the spokes meet, is called the henhouse. The design is a masterpiece that is not too complicated and yet provides several paths for running and is perfect for playing "Fox and Geese."

As students arrive, they are careful not to disturb Gene's outdoor art and enter the school for their morning classes. At 10:15 am Miss No Mistakes reminds them that if they are going outside they need to be dressed warmly and to be sure to wear their boots. She dismisses the classes and watches the students rush to the cloakroom to throw on their winter coats and caps and struggle with their overshoes. That is, everyone but Jenny, who is a second grader and receives straight A's. She often stays indoors to help the teacher tidy up the classroom. The rest of the students disappear out the door into the dazzling sunlight and bright snow shouting, "Who gets to be the Fox?"

"Let me. Let me!" yell the ten students in unison.

"Not you, you always chase me first." "The boys always get to be the Fox." "It's got to a girl this time." "Never in my life have I ever been the Fox," is the mixture of hollering coming from the noisy youngsters, ages five through thirteen.

"It should be Gene," shouts Vincent.

Jimmy chimes in, "I agree; he got here early to make the circles."

Everyone accepts the suggestion, although somewhat reluctantly that Gene will be the Fox. The remaining students will be geese. As they enter the circular configuration, the geese run to the center of the circle, the hen house, and Gene waits standing on the outer rim.

When everyone is in the center, Gene calls out, "Geese, geese, how many geese are here today?"

"More than you can catch and carry away," taunt the geese.

The fox charges toward the hen house on one of the paths. The geese flee the hen house, running on different paths and attempting to avoid the fox. The game of tag is in full flight. When a goose is caught, it returns to the hen house and stays there until all the geese are captured. The last goose tagged becomes the new fox, and a new game begins. Jimmy is the last goose caught seconds before the end of recess and becomes the new fox when the game begins at noon. Jimmy and Gene are both late returning from recess and receive the usual stern look from Miss No Mistakes.

They play the game at noon, but by the end of the afternoon recess two students have wandered off and are making a snowman beside the partially snow-covered merry-go-round. Marilyn, who was never the fox, is making snow angels, and Vincent is calling for everyone to return to the game, but the game has lost its novelty.

The following morning Jimmy tries to bring new life to the old game and introduces a variation. He combines the game of tag with throwing snowballs. In the new game, the fox doesn't actually have to touch a goose but can tag someone by hitting the goose with a snowball. Before the end of noon on the second day, a full blown snow fight has resulted in total disorder. In addition, many have chapped hands from playing in the snow and are returning to the school house to warm up. Marilyn is crying because she never got to be the fox; and Miss No Mistakes is upset with all of the noise, energy, and snow brought into her classroom.

At the end of the second day, Gene leaves school and looks back over his shoulder. He realizes that the magic of the snowy field with its carefully crafted circles has disappeared. It will be school as normal tomorrow unless the three musketeers – Jimmy, Vincent and he – can introduce some excitement.

This year on March 1, Bristol 2 doesn't lose students but gains three, bringing the total to thirteen. A family, with a boy named Paul who is four years younger than Gene, moves in to a farm house that is next to Gene's home. Paul is solidly built, has blond hair, blue eyes, and is fair skinned. He is full of energy and athletic; since he is only seven Gene doesn't pay much attention to him.

The Smith family moves into a home that has been vacant for six months and is a mile north of the school. The Smiths have two students: Art who has coal black hair, talks too much, and is two years older than Gene and his sister Karla who is two years younger than Gene. She flirts with the boys and wants to play with them. Gene doesn't know much about girls, but he thinks she is boy crazy, something he has heard about but has never witnessed.

The first Saturday in March, Gene and Jimmy ask Art to walk to Hardin Creek with them to see if all the ice has broken up and if the water is running again. Sometimes there is a March ice jam, which causes flooding in the low lying areas. The two boys compete to be among the first to spread the word that the creek is backing up. They expect Art to consider it an honor to be asked to go with them.

"You guys got girlfriends?" Art asks as they begin their walk.

"No," they answer in unison. Both boys believe that having a girlfriend would be embarrassing.

"I do; I got a couple," Art brags.

"Good for you," Jimmy replies and then adds, "I guess."

"Yeah, at my last school, all the girls wanted me to kiss them and touch them, you know," Art boasts.

"I hope the ice is broken up," Gene says, trying to change the topic.

"Girls like to kiss and mess around," says Art as if he is a real lover-boy. He then begins to lecture them about sex. The two friends find his lecture as humorous as it is untrue.

"That isn't true," states Gene. "Fooling around with girls can lead to trouble."

"Well, I don't get in trouble."

"My dad says that only fools are foolish enough to fool around with girls," chimes in Jimmy.

"Art, I raise rabbits, and I know that when rabbits fool around they have baby rabbits," Gene boasts with some authority,

"Same thing is true with cows, but they have calves," laughs Jimmy. "I guess you just haven't been around much, Art."

"Are you accusing me of lying?" Art replies, giving a menacing look at the two friends.

"No, he isn't accusing you of being a liar, just dumb," interjects Gene.

"You guys are babies. Come to me when you grow up and want to learn what to do with girls," replies Art as he turns and heads home.

Calling Art dumb isn't a good way to start a friendship, and the following week Art begins slugging Gene in the upper arm, asking him, "How's the rabbit boy?"

"Stop hitting me or I'll..."

"Or what? Get your buddy to beat me up?" interrupts Art.

The two avoid Art whenever possible. But Art zeros in on Gene and continues to punch his arm causing the arm to bruise, or Art pinches him when he passes his desk and whispers, "Rabbit Boy," or "Genie Weenie."

Jimmy escapes the bullying maybe because he is in awe of Art's sister Karla, but he also avoids Art when he's on the playground. Or maybe Art only wants to torment one person at a time. Whatever the reason for the harassment, Gene is determined not to let the bullying make him hide or stop from playing at recess. He is old enough, big enough, and smart enough to stop Art's harassment. He just doesn't know when or exactly how he is going to do it.

On the last day of school, there is the traditional picnic for the students and their mothers. Fathers are invited, but planting corn keeps the dads from going to the school picnic.

Miss No Mistakes is not returning to teach next fall, and Gene is delighted. Jimmy discovers that she is as frightened of spring storms as she is of snow storms. Whenever storm clouds appear in the west, Jimmy predicts a tornado, and all the students head for the storm cellar. The boys joke that maybe she is leaving because she doesn't want to risk being sucked up by an Iowa tornado. And after discovering her Achilles' heel, the students see threatening tornados whenever there is a spring thunderstorm. The month of April can be riddled with rain storms, but only a few actually harbor a tornado. Nevertheless, during April the fifteen students huddle in the dark storm cave and pretend to be frightened as rain splashes against the cellar door on five different occasions. And once the rain stops, the youngsters scamper out of the damp cave and hurry into the school smiling at each other – another afternoon with no classes.

Today is the ideal day for the end-of-the-year picnic. There's a bright sun, a gentle breeze, and no storm clouds. The mothers arrive about 11 am bringing potato salads, deviled eggs, baked beans, hot dogs, and lots of lemonade.

Jenny's mother, wearing a sleeveless sundress, suggests, "We should eat inside. A gust of wind could blow some dust in our food."

"What's a picnic without some dirt?" whispers Jimmy.

"Don't say anything," Gene murmurs. "If we eat inside our mothers won't bugs us about how to play baseball."

"Good thinking," Jimmy replies.

After lunch Jenny remains inside with Miss No Mistakes and the mothers while the twelve remaining students rush outside to begin a game of 'work-up'. Work-up is like playing baseball, but without teams. Alternating by age, youngest then oldest, the students choose a position to play. Today there will be four at bat, and the remaining eight will fill in the field positions with no shortstop. A batter continues to bat until he or she is out, then that player goes to right field and everyone moves up. Right fielder to center field, the center field player moves to left field, the left field player to third base, third baseman to second base, and so on until the pitcher moves to become the catcher. The former catcher becomes the new batter.

When the game begins, Art pokes fun at Gene, "Does the rabbit boy hop around the baseball diamond?"

When Art is pitching and Gene is at bat, Art throws the ball at Gene's head. "Why can't you hit the ball Genie Weenie? You're so smart."

"Throw it like a real pitcher and I'll show you," shouts Gene.

The two banter as the rest of the students howl, "Play ball." Gene strikes out, and the game resumes somewhat quietly until Art is at bat and Gene is first baseman. Art hits a high fly that is dropped by Paul. Art races to the first base and needlessly slides into the flat rock used as the base. Brushing himself off, he starts chanting:

"Gene, Gene made a machine.

Joe, Joe made it go,

Art, Art let a fart,

and blew it apart."

"You can't hit a ball and everything you make falls apart," sneers the older boy.

Gene trying not to cry, shouts back, "Stop it Art! I'm sick of you."

"Make me stop, rabbit boy."

Without warning, Gene hits him. It's not a soft warning thump, but a real sucker punch. It's like when Gene smacks the cows in their stomachs when they refuse to move. Or like his outburst in the boxing ring. He doesn't aim at Art's stomach; he aims at his face. The blow lands on Art's nose. Taken by surprise, Art feels his nose and sees blood on his hand. His eyes begin to swell up with tears.

Gene stands firm, waiting for a fight. The students freeze and remain silent. Blood begins to drip from Art's nose, and tears trickle down his cheeks. Gene clinches his teeth and utters, "Don't make fun of me."

Art, surprised and stunned, swaggers off the field. He doesn't walk toward the school house because he'd have to explain the bloody nose; he heads home. Art isn't sure how many more punches Gene has left in him, and, already disgraced, he doesn't want to make it worse.

There is no cheering, no congratulations, and no criticism; but the game is over. The only comment is from Gene's buddy Jimmy, "Man that game of work-up really got you worked up." They lock arms and begin their walk home. School is over for another year, and next fall there will be a new teacher. Gene has all summer to forget about Art.

Gene's dad is anxious to return to his spring field work, and now that the rain has stopped the ground will be dry enough and the corn tall enough to cultivate in two days. The tips of the new corn are piercing the soil in search of sunlight. A checkerboard design, common across Iowa, is taking shape in the newly planted corn fields. There is enough work to keep a squadron of soldiers busy around the farm. Gene's two older brothers are repairing fences, and his dad is preparing the brooder house where a hundred baby chicks will be kept. All of the chicks will be kept in the brooder house until the males are separated from the females. The young hens will be moved to the chicken house where they will contribute to the farm income by laying eggs to be sold and the money used for buying groceries and home supplies. The young roosters remain in the brooder house until they are of fryer size and then butchered and placed in the freezer to be enjoyed next winter. There is an endless list of tasks that farmers must complete every spring, and everyone on the farm learns there are no eight hour work days.

"Gene, I need you to take these cultivator blades to Charlie in Farlin to be sharpened. As soon as it dries out, I'll be cultivating corn." His dad hands him twelve blades tied together in two bundles with baling wire.

"Okay," Gene jumps on the old wobbly bicycle, which was handed down to him from his oldest brother. Gene dreams about the day when he will be able to buy a new bike, but he hasn't saved enough money, so a new bike will wait. It's a two mile ride to Farlin on the gravel road. The blacksmith is out of the shop, and Gene isn't to leave the shovels there without explaining what he wants. He goes next door to the pool hall to see if Charlie is there.

When he enters the pool room, Mike, owner of the grocery store, and Jimmy's dad are talking. "Hi, young fella," Mike calls to Gene. "Did you come in for a game of pool?"

"Not today. I'm on an errand: I brought the cultivator blades in for sharpening. Dad is in a hurry to get into the fields."

"Your dad always wants to be the first to complete his field work," adds Jimmy's dad.

"Old Charlie just stepped out and will be back soon. You can practice your pool until he returns if you like," offers Mike.

Gene aligns the cue ball with the eight ball and hits it softly, as Charlie has taught him. He continues practicing, taking easy shots, and then racks up the balls once the table is cleared. The two men talk about Otto, a soldier who recently returned home.

"He just kind of went bonkers."

"My wife says his mother told her that he is either crying or fighting. It is especially bad whenever he drinks booze."

"The war did it. It's shellshock. Before he went to war, he was a gentle eighteen year old kid. Never a fighter; he wouldn't even hold the pigs when it was time to castrate them."

"Yeah, it's too damn bad. He got to Europe just in time for the Battle of the Bulge, and the fighting must have messed him up pretty good."

"He'll be OK once he comes back from Clarinda. The doctors there will help him. Otto's a nice kid. But with May upon us, he better get better soon or he won't be of much help for his dad."

Old Charlie returns from an errand in Jefferson. Seeing Gene he asks, "Why aren't you home helping your dad?"

"I am helping; I've got some plow blades for you to sharpen. Dad's getting anxious to cultivate."

"There goes your dad. He's always in a hurry to get his spring work done. I can have these sharpened by tomorrow at noon."

Otto is the second guy in the county that Gene has heard about who is suffering from shellshock. Gerald, a friend of the family, talks very little now. Before the war he talked his fool head off, according to Gene's dad.

Riding his bike home, he spots a goldfinch playing on a cattail that withstood the winter winds and hears a meadowlark in the hayfields. The war seems like a long time ago, but hearing about Otto has got him thinking about the war. No one talks about it now; the newspaper focuses on new jobs, the recovery in Europe, and the Russians and Americans disagreeing on just about everything. He glides into the lane and skids to a stop just in time to join the family for lunch. There will be time later to think; he now needs to eat and then clean out the rabbit pens. His mom has been after him to have everything clean when the first bunnies arrive.

Gene cleans the rabbit hutches and leaves the buck and doe alone for a few minutes to start his 1947 family of rabbits. He returns and notices flies gathering around the fence to feast on the rabbit droppings. He would like to rid the rabbit area of flies and goes to the barn to borrow the hand sprayer filled with the insecticide DDT. It is advertised as a mild poison and is replacing the long fly strips for killing flies.

Prior to the end of World War II, long sticky ribbons hung from the barn ceiling where the cows were milked. The flies flew into the sticky ribbons or landed on them and became stuck. There they died, and when the streamers become satiated with dead flies the strips were discarded with the manure. The strips caught the flies before landing on the cows, and fewer flies reduced the amount of tail wagging making the cows more contented and make milking more comfortable. However, some flies escaped the sticky ribbons and continued to sting the cows.

Gene's dad has been replacing the strips by using DDT spray to rid the barn of flies. The spray kills all the flies in the barn, and the flies can't avoid the insecticide mist. Gene reasons that if it kills the flies in the barn it should also kill flies around the rabbit pens. He retrieves the circular canister spray can from the barn and carries it to the rabbit hutches. There, he starts pumping the handle, spraying a mist around the rabbits. His mom sees him spraying the DDT around the rabbit hutches and asks, "What are you doing with the DDT?"

"I'm killing flies that gather there," replies Gene.

"Be careful using that poison," cautions his mom. "They used it during the war to control the mosquitoes and lice, especially in the tropical climates. But I'm not so sure it is as safe as everyone is saying."

"It keeps the flies from biting the cows when we're milking."

"But the warning on the DDT cans says to keep it away from all food and away from house plants and pets. Maybe you shouldn't use it on your rabbits."

"These aren't pets," Gene replies.

"That isn't the point. Companies who make DDT aren't really sure what it does kill besides insects. You don't want to harm your rabbits, especially the bunnies."

Gene isn't convinced his mom knows what she is talking about, but he returns the hand- operated canister to the shelf in the barn.

———

Gene's dad is the school's director and had hired Miss No Mistakes, but since she isn't returning he needs to find a new teacher. Since the end of the war, elementary teachers are more available – the factory jobs are being filled by veterans returning from the military. His dad hires Mrs. Williams.

She's middle aged, wears glasses, and styles her graying hair into a bun. Her nose sometimes turns slightly red, especially when a student is about to receive a lecture. Gene hears his dad tell his mom that the school is fortunate to hire Mrs. Williams. She worked in a Waterloo war plant during the war and has returned to Greene County to teach. She has teaching experience and hopefully will remain at Bristol 2 for more than one or two years. She will continue to teach in the one room school until it is finally closed in 1959. Gene benefits from her teaching and guidance for his sixth, seventh, and eighth grades at Bristol 2.

He and Jimmy don't want the new teacher to think that they are goody-two-shoes, or she might expect more work from them. They welcome her on the first school day by placing several small toads on her desk when she leaves to ring the noon bell. The toads hop to the floor as soon as the two boys return to their desks, and as students hurry in from the playground the toads are accidentally trampled on by the stampede of students. The little toads never had a chance. Gene glances at Jimmy and receives a devious smile in return. They know they are in for some unusual punishment if she discovers they are the ones that brought in the toads. The two boys sit straight up in their desks and focus on the United States flag in a corner away from the squashed reptiles.

"Oh my, oh my shoes," shrieks Jenny looking at her new shoes that are sprinkled with toad guts.

"Ack. Makes me what to throw-up," interjects Paul, pretending to vomit.

Mrs. Williams in her black print dress, wearing medium high heels, and with perfectly combed hair returns to the room. She looks at the disgusting sight and quietly asks Jimmy and Gene to clean up the sorry-looking mess. There is no outrage, no screaming – nothing but a quiet firm voice giving directions. Her voice has a tone that leaves no room for an argument. Her experience as line supervisor at the war plant in Waterloo, Iowa, is useful even in a one-room rural school. In silence Jimmy and Gene clean up the toad's entrails as she returns to her desk and waits for the classroom to return to normal before they recite the Pledge of Allegiance.

The next day the two boys place a tack on her chair. Again there is no crisis. She merely walks to her desk, picks up the tack and places it in her desk drawer. She is not only a teacher, but teaches maturity by behaving as an adult. Her behavior demonstrates that it is not necessary to shout to make a point.

Gene seldom did any extra credit work for Miss No Mistakes. He completed his assignments quickly and used his extra time visiting with Jimmy or Vincent. He wasn't allowed to do the extra work unless he redid the assignments with no erasures or cross-outs, so it was easier for him to do an average job than to do a perfect job and, therefore, escaped extra work.

Mrs. Williams approaches Gene differently. She expects questions to be answered correctly and turned in on time, but neatness isn't essential for him to do extra projects. And she has projects waiting for him after the regular assignments are completed. She doesn't expect learning just to happen. Vincent's dad tells Gene and Jimmy, "Mrs. Williams isn't teaching by guess or by golly. She is going to make you guys students."

This new teacher encourages reading books and writing a report to earn extra credit. Gene begins to understand that learning is more than just doing the assignments, and since he enjoys reading he reads as much as he can. His reading expands beyond *Superman, Wonder Woman, Archie* and the *Green Lantern*. He is now reading the *Bobbsey Twins Adventures* and the *Hardy Boys Mysteries*.

A clean school is important to Mrs. Williams and she believes it is not just the responsibility of the teacher and Jenny; it's everyone's responsibility. On Friday afternoons before leaving school, Jimmy, Art, and Gene sprinkle green or red sweeping compound on the wooden floorboards and sweep the oil-soaked sawdust across the floor. The compound absorbs the dirt brought into the classroom during the week by the lively youngsters. After sweeping up the compound, it leaves an oily finish on the weathered pine flooring. Paul, Vincent, Karla, and Marilyn erase the slate chalkboards and clean the erasers by pounding them on the front steps. They sometimes draw pictures on the steps with the small pieces of chalk that are being discarded.

Seeing the steps, Jimmy declares, "The patterns and drawings look like a Monet."

"Maybe more like a Picasso abstraction," expounds Paul.

"They certainly don't look like a Norman Rockwell," offers Gene as he critiques the harmless chalk graffiti, which remains on the school steps until it's washed away by rain. The students know there are different painters because Mrs. Williams introduces an art class that is more than cutting and pasting. Weekly, she presents large copies of famous paintings and discusses the artists with the upper grade students.

At the end of the month, the students do more than sweep the floor and clean the chalkboard. They wash the slate chalkboards and windowsills. They cleanse their desks with soap and water that has been heated in a cast iron teapot that rests on top of the coal-burning potbelly stove. The hot water provides humidity in the classroom and hot water for maintenance tasks.

Art, now in eighth grade, struts around the classroom, talking more than actually working, but the students have accepted his swaggering and talking without saying or doing much. But there is one job that even Art wants to do – fetch water.

After Mrs. Williams gives her spirited pep talk about accepting responsibility, Art, Jimmy, and Gene want to get water. They see it as a sign of maturity and an opportunity to leave the school house and get fresh air. Gaining the boys' willingness, she assigns the task to the three boys. A schedule is drawn up and posted by the automatic water fountain. Mrs. Williams brought with her a new drinking fountain. It's a bubble fountain. When water is poured into the ceramic bowl, the students can push a small metal button, and water is dispersed through a bubbler that students can drink without ever touching the container or using a cup. This is a big improvement over the pail of water with a community dipper that Gene first used as a primary student.

The water duty schedule is posted in the entrance area and updated every week. Alongside the schedule are the instructions

1. Introduce yourself to the farmer or his wife.
2. Request permission before you pump water in the bucket.
3. Do not waste time going or returning from getting water.
4. Do not throw stones at cows in the pastures. (This was added after Jimmy was reported to have been throwing rocks at some of the cows.

First week in the month – Art
Second week in the month – Gene
Third week in the month – Jimmy
Fourth week in the month – assigned to the student who has no outstanding assignments.

Gene is anxious for the second week to arrive, so he can fetch water. On Monday he arrives early to carry the empty two-gallon pail to the closest farmhouse. After obtaining permission, he pumps the pail full of water, secures the lid to keep water from sloshing on his jeans, and returns to school. He doesn't see getting the water as a chore or as a discipline measure; it is a valued service. He sometimes takes longer than Mrs. Williams expects and is asked what took him so long. It is usually because he is visiting with the farmer about the weather or crops. He isn't reprimanded but advised to attend to the job and save the visiting for after school. Soon he knows the local farmers and their wives and is seen as trustworthy, dependable, and someone who might be hired to cut cockleburs out of the corn.

Sweeping floors, washing desks, cleaning chalkboards, and fetching water are all part of the curriculum; and responsibility becomes the fourth R taught by Mrs. Williams.

Mrs. Williams encourages Gene to read more, but finding books is a challenge. An old book case in the rear of the classroom holds the school's library. The new teacher has contributed some books like *The Bobbsey Twins Solve a Mystery The Bobbsey Twins at the Carnival,* and a few *Hardy Boy Mysteries*, but there are few classics. *Heidi, Little Women, Little Men, Uncle Tom's Cabin,* and several old history and mathematics text books are available. There is also a dog-eared dictionary and a 1939 World Atlas. Protected on the lower two shelves are two sets of encyclopedias, the *Americana* with maroon colored covers and an older less used *Britannia* with tattered black covers.

The students keep the encyclopedias separated according to the binding's color, but the books are seldom in alphabetical order. The *Americana* volumes with information about the American Revolution and Iowa are missing. And relying on the *Britannia* for information about the American Revolutionary War is like asking Gene's Grandma Millard about the Civil War. She was raised in Missouri and declares there was nothing civil about that war. She calls it The War Between the States and never forgave the US Government for their treatment of the Missourians. The *Britannia* set is complete and intact but more difficult to read.

In the fall of 1947, a county-wide traveling library is started, which increases the availability of books to the students attending rural schools. The county school superintendent visits Bristol 2 every two weeks with his trunk full of library books. Students are permitted to check out two books and return them on his next visit.

With sensitive and patient guidance, Mrs. Williams expands Gene's reading options. He becomes friends with all of the little women, Kim, Jim Hawkins, and Billy Bones, and floats down the Mississippi with Huck Finn and Tom Sawyer. Reading about their adventures is almost as enjoyable as when he and Jimmy played in the Hardin Creek. Gene's surplus energy is directed toward reading adventurous books, which reduces his involvement in disturbances.

The traveling school library isn't the only new service. In October of 1947, the Bristol 2 mothers meet at the school to discuss an idea suggested by the home economist from the Greene County Extension Office.

She tells the mothers, "Hot lunch programs have been available in large cities, and the US Government passed legislation last year making hot lunches permanent for most school districts in the United States." She stops and waits for a response. Hearing none, she continues, "Bristol Township is not participating in the program because of lack of personnel, but it is still appropriate to provide the students with a balanced and healthy noon lunch." She stops again for any reaction from the mothers.

"We could fix a warm meal and bring it to school before noon," Gene's mother suggests.

"Like what kind of food?" asks Art's mother.

"Chili is a good choice. It has meat, beans, tomatoes," offers Paul's mom.

"I can fix mashed potatoes covered with hot creamed corn. My Art loves that," suggests his mom.

"Every kid likes biscuits covered with creamed dried beef or creamy ground hamburger gravy. And I can open canned beans from last summer and bake fresh cookies to go with it," states Gene's mom.

Jenny's mom had been silent during the discussion.

"Do you think Jenny would enjoy a hot meal?" asks Jimmy's mom.

"Yes, and I can always send an apple and sandwich if she doesn't like what is served."

"Good! And when it's your turn you can fix Jenny's favorite lunch to share with the other students."

It is agreed by the Bristol 2 moms to form a lunch program. The county home economist is pleased and leaves the school. The first lunch is to be delivered the first week in November.

Gene, Jimmy, and Vincent are anxious for their first meal to arrive. Will there be enough for everyone? Will it taste OK? But their concerns cease when the spicy chili aroma fills the classroom as Jimmy's mom delivers the chili with cheese and crackers. A daily procession of noon meals including hotdogs, loose beef sandwiches, and Art's mom's starchy potatoes and creamed corn continue until March 1. At that time the students return to bringing their own lunches or walking home for soup at noon until the following November when the meals on wheels lunches resume.

Gene's interest in cowboy movies hasn't stopped, but it has lessened. In the fall of 1947 he attends a movie, *The Yearling*, with his cousin Goldie. The movie is about a boy living in Florida who adopts a fawn as his pet after his pa kills the fawn's mother. The boy, Jody, becomes attached to the fawn but at the end he is forced to kill his own pet after it is shot.

Returning to school the following Monday, Gene discusses the movie with his teacher.

"It's the best movie I've seen."

"The movie is based on a book that won a Pulitzer Prize for the best novel in 1939."

"I didn't know it was a book. Are the movie and the book the same?" Gene asks.

"If you read the book, you can decide for yourself."

The following Thursday Mr. Morris delivers the book to Gene from the Greene County Traveling Library. Gene enjoys reading about Florida's backwoods wilderness, and he understands Jody's parents and the relatives who live in town. He likes the book because it provides more scenes than can be shown in the movie.

Another 1947 movie *Cynthia*, starring a young Elizabeth Taylor, gives Gene his first crush on a movie starlet. He tells his mother about the young sickly girl who rebels against her parents, receives her first kiss, and falls in love.

"Do you think she's pretty?" asks his mom.

"She is pretty," he reveals to his mom.

Gene's mother realizing that Gene is often idealistic and romantic suggests the family attend the movie, *The Best Years of Our Lives*. Gene has asked his mom about returning soldiers that he heard about at Farlin. He wants to know why they drink too much, abuse their families, and become depressed. She believes the post World War II movie will provide him with a practical view of the world, and an opportunity to see the consequences and scars left on returning veterans.

After seeing the movie, Gene and his mom discuss the sailor who lost his hands in a fire aboard his ship and is left with an artificial hand, the pilot who has reoccurring nightmares about combat, and the third man who drinks to forget the war. His mother doesn't take pleasure in discussing the dark side of war, but she believes a dose of reality is needed to balance a diet of idealism.

For Christmas Gene receives an Erector Set, a gift that is practical and sensible, and will keep him busy and entertained. Throughout vacation he plays with the metal strips and gears from his set, and occasionally constructs bizarre looking skyscrapers and strange homes, using a combination of items from the Erector Set, and logs from his younger brother's box of Lincoln Logs. These structures reflect the modern world because of the metal pieces, and an earlier time is seen in the buildings made from the Lincoln Logs.

The Best Years of Our Lives, and The Yearling were 1946 Academy Award contenders. Gene sees the movies a year later, but attending a movie a year after it is released is not unusual, and Gene doesn't attend the Christmas classic *It's a Wonderful Life* in 1946 or 1947. However the movies he does attend provide a balance between reality and dreams, something which Gene's mom believes is necessary.

Fortunately, there are reminders from the world around him to bring him back to reality. The world atlas he receives from his Uncle

Frank at Christmas is such a reminder. It identifies the new countries that are created after World War II, and their names don't match the names of countries that Gene finds on the maps at school. He studies his new atlas and imagines what the people in those countries look like.

1948

"Did you enjoy Christmas?" Mrs. Williams asks the students once they are seated and the pledge recited.

Vincent quickly replies, "We had the chicken pox. Want to see my scab?"

The students laugh; everyone but Jenny, who thinks it is gross to even talk about pox or scabs let alone look at one.

"I spent the vacation in the house with a cold, coughing most the time," volunteers Jimmy. "But I got a Red Ryder BB gun. Mom says I can only shoot at tin cans."

"My Uncle gave me a world atlas that shows the new countries," Gene shares.

"What new countries?" asks Marilyn?

"All of the countries created after the war," answers Gene, looking disgusted because of her lack of knowledge.

During World War II, Gene develops a curiosity and interest in Okinawa, Midway, Stalingrad, the Philippines, and about any place where battles were fought. The 1939 globe that Gene enjoyed earlier is now kept in the storage area along with old textbooks, but he still enjoys learning about world geography and current events.

Mrs. Williams is always searching for projects to keep the two boys busy, because without an activity they create something to do their own. Jimmy needs to keep his hands busy while Gene needs to keep his head busy. January is a good month to start new projects, especially if they stay involved in the venture until spring.

She approaches Jimmy after he has consumed a plate of mashed potatoes covered with creamed hamburger and green beans from the hot lunch program.

"Jimmy, if you go to my car, you'll find some lumber, nails, and a tool box. Please bring them inside."

"I'm on my way."

When Jimmy returns, she examines some blue prints with him for building a display easel and asks him to construct the easel after his regular assignments are completed.

"Hammering must be done in the storage area away from the classroom," she emphasizes and then approaches Gene.

"This morning you told us about the world atlas you received for Christmas. Would you bring it to school, so we can use it in studying about the United Nations?"

"Sure," replies Gene. "But why study the United Nations?"

"They're involved in lots of international activities. Last November the UN voted to partition Palestine into two states, one Jewish and one Arab. You can look for articles in the newspaper and write a special report about the UN and report to the class next month when we share current events. Jimmy is building an easel for displaying materials, and you may want to use it in giving your report.

Gene begins that evening by asking his dad about the United Nations. His dad explains there was the League of Nations, but countries didn't support it and before long the countries were fighting among themselves. The Greene County School Traveling Library arrives on Friday, and Gene asks the county school superintendent if he has any books on the United Nations.

Mr. Morris returns in two weeks with several books about the UN. Gene learns that the twenty-six nations that were at war with Germany met in 1942 and agreed not to sign separate peace agreements with Germany. The agreement is the beginning of the United Nations. He also learns that there are many issues for the United Nations to resolve and that the world is upside down following the collapse of Germany and Japan. The British Commonwealth is breaking up. India is fighting for its independence. There is a war in French Indochina. European Jews are seeking to live in the newly created Israel. Germany is split into two countries: West Germany which is occupied by the Americans, French, and British; and East Germany occupied by the Russians. Japan is occupied by the United States.

The current events project keeps Gene busy through January and February. Art isn't bothering Gene since he is studying for the eighth grade test and stays after school with Mrs. Williams to review possible questions. He needs to pass the test to graduate and go on to high school.

On the first Friday of March, Gene reports to the students about the United Nations. He uses the new easel that Jimmy built, displaying maps that show the trouble spots and a date line showing the development of the United Nations. Karla helps him place the maps on the display board as Gene reads his report. With the projects completed, the two boys become restless and begin horsing around again

---

The year before Mrs. Williams arrived; Gene and Jimmy were playing catch with a baseball in the schoolhouse during recess. Miss No Mistakes thought it was better for them to play catch with one another than to organize an indoor baseball game that involved everyone.

The two frequently threw the ball at each other rather than to each other. If they couldn't catch the ball, they let it bounce off the slate blackboard. In one of these games of catch, Gene threw a wild pitch at Jimmy, and the ball crashed into the chalkboard, breaking it and leaving a four-inch jagged hole in the blackboard. Slate blackboards are heavy and not easily replaced, so nothing was done to repair it. The gaping hole is usually covered with a guide for punctuation or a list of good sportsmanship rules.

Where Did All the Cowboys Go?

Mrs. Williams stops the two from playing catch indoors. However, she can't prevent eleven year old boys from doing what they do best – grab-ass. On a March afternoon with a heavy wet snow falling outside, Jimmy and Gene are confined to playing a game of "touched you last." There are no rules or redeeming qualities to the game. The game is played with you touch me, I touch you, you touch me, I touch you. Each time, they make the next contact a little harder. Finally Jimmy pushes Gene hard enough to cause him to stumble backward. To break his fall, Gene grabs at the slate chalkboard and pushes his hand into the broken opening. Gene pulls his hand from the blackboard cavity to discover a two-inch cut on his left hand and an inch of slate sticking out from below his little finger. Mrs. Williams removes the piece of slate and blood rushes out of the wound. Jenny, seeing the gushing blood begins to cry.

Jimmy is sniveling, "I'm sorry, I'm sorry, I didn't mean it."

Unable to stop the bleeding, Mrs. Williams wraps the hand in gauze and sends Gene home to see if his dad or mom needs to take him to the doctor's office.

At home his dad examines the cut. His dad is a pretty good doctor. He pulls out baby teeth if they don't come out by themselves, removes slivers, and bandages cuts and burns. And he gets lots of practice raising four boys. For such emergencies he needs a pan of hot water, soap, a bottle of Watkins Liniment, some gauze and tape. The patient bites down and hopes that the pain goes away. His dad washes out the wound with warm soapy water, removes a few small pieces of slate with his tweezers and tells Gene, "This is going to hurt a little." With no more warning, he pours Watkins Liniment over the injury. He tapes the cut shut with three small strips of tape and places a clean bandage over the wound. The entire palm of the hand is wrapped with gauze and tape. "No need to bother a doctor with this one; you might as well go back to school," instructs his dad.

The March snow has stopped as Gene walks back to school, but he can see red speckles and blood stains left on the fresh snow. The bright red spots against the white snow are interesting and out of place. Less than an hour ago the blood was in his body; now it's an abstract drawing in the snow. He looks at the wrapped hand and feels the throbbing across the palm as he opens the school house door.

The students are singing "Alouette," a French Canadian folk song that is used to warm up before they start practicing the songs for the eighth grade county graduation ceremony. The students stop singing, and Mrs. Williams asks Gene if he is feeling well enough to sing. He nods his head yes and steps next to Jimmy who tells him, "I'm really sorry. I guess we got too rough."

"That's okay. Dad fixed it," Gene replies with a grin.

The students resume singing, and Gene joins in, singing as loud as he can to take his mind off of the throbbing.

The chalkboard accident is a result of natural consequences. Like his parents tell him, "If you horse around, you're likely to get hurt." After the incident there are no threats of lawsuits and no grudges. Gene's dad continues to replace the bandage for the next few weeks. The swelling goes down, the infection lessens, and the wound heals, concealing a tiny speck of slate that didn't get washed out by his dad's medical procedure.

―――

There isn't an organized physical education program at Bristol 2, but playing games serves as the PE program and selecting games for children ages five through thirteen is difficult. The best games are those where older students can look out for the younger students, be played by all students, and fit into a fifteen minute recess that requires little equipment. Work-Up is a good spring game and Fox and Geese a good winter game, but the students are always searching for new games.

"What can we play now?" is Vincent's ongoing question.

"Ask your parents what games they played when they were young," suggests Mrs. Williams. Next week you can report back and play those games. Accepting her challenge, the students return the following week to report on their parents' favorite games.

Paul's mom liked to play *Red Rover.* It's played with two teams in an open field. Team members hold on to each other's hands tightly and take turns in calling out "Red Rover, Red Rover send (name of a student) right over." The student whose name is called runs as fast as possible toward the other team, hoping to break the opposing team's grip on each other's hand. If the student breaks through the line, the person returns to their team; if not, the student becomes a member of that team. The game doesn't end until only one student remains on the opposing team.

Gene's dad liked playing *Anti Over.* This game is played with a softball, and the students divide into two teams. One team takes the ball and goes to one side of the school house. The other team occupies the opposite side and is the receiving team. The team with the ball has a member throw the ball over the building and all the team hollers "Anti Over." If the ball fails to make it over the building, everyone calls out "Pig Tail," and another attempt is made to throw the ball over the school calling out once again "Anti Over." Members of that team attempt to catch the ball when it makes it over the building. If the ball is caught, one team member takes the ball, and all members sneak around the building. The team that is treading softly around the school house must use expert undercover techniques, for they hope to surprise the opposing team. The person with the ball tags as many members of the opposing team as possible before they escape to the other side. Those tagged become members of the team that caught the ball. Students not tagged and who make it half way around the school are now given their chance to catch the ball when it is thrown to them. Throwing the ball back and forth and conducting sneak attacks continues until all students end up on the same team.

"Those games sound too rough," chimes in Jenny. "I want to play *Mother May I*? My mother says its lots of fun."

"How do we play it?" asks Vincent.

"I'll show you."

The students go outside to the playground.

"Everyone line up in the middle of the field," directs Jenny in her high nasal voice. She then retreats about seventy feet from the line of students.

She starts the game by saying, "Karla, take two giant steps," and explains that after each request the student must ask, "May I?"

Karla answers, "May I?"

Jenny gives her permission, and Karla takes two huge steps.

"Vincent, take one duck step," requests Jenny and demonstrates that is a squat and walk step.

"May I?" asks Vincent.

"Yes, you may," Jenny answers in a soft voice.

"For gosh sakes how long does this game last?" shouts Jimmy.

"Jimmy, take four baby steps." directs Jenny. Jimmy immediately takes four small steps. "You forgot to say May I. You must go back to the line," instructs Jenny.

"For gosh sakes," argues Jimmy.

The game continues with Jenny calling out to individual students to take giant steps, baby steps, duck steps, and alligator steps. The alligator steps require the players to lie down and stretch their arms out as far as possible and then stand to claim one alligator step. Students can creep forward, but if the Mother, Jenny in today's game, catches them cheating they must return to the starting line.

"Let's hear about another game," pleads Jimmy.

Vincent's favorite is *King of the Mountain*. In this game a student claims the top of the storm cave as his kingdom. Other students try to knock him off the top of the cave. When the king is knocked off, there is a new king until that king is pushed off. It is more like wrestling without rules than a game, and often someone ends up crying. Karla is the only girl who plays the game and that is because she likes wrestling with the boys. Jenny finds the game disgusting.

Crack the Whip is a popular game on windy days. There is no reason for its popularity on windy days, except it is unpredictable like the wind.

The students line up and take hold of each other's hand. The leader of the line runs as fast as possible with those behind him holding hands and running. The leader stops and swings the person hanging on to him. This starts a chain reaction, and the player on the end must hang on tightly. If the end player loses his or her grip and is flung away, the leader takes the end position.

The second person becomes the new leader. There is no end to the game, and it keeps grinding on with students hollering and shouting.

King of the Mountain and *Crack the Whip* result in more bruised knees and skinned elbows than the other games. When a student get injured, another student helps clean the cuts with soap and water, and if there is blood a little Watkins Liniment is dabbed on the injury. A bandage is usually placed over the wound to identify where the injury took place.

The games provide students with exercise, teaches them the importance of good sportsmanship, and gives them basic first aid training.

———

Art leaves Gene along throughout the year, and unlike last year, when Gene bloodied his nose, the school year ends with no memorable events. Art passes his eighth grade exam and will be attending high school next fall.

As summer begins, Gene and Jimmy resume their fishing and swimming in the Hardin Creek but less often. Gene is now working more around the farm, and one of his new jobs is to cut the undergrowth along the fence rows. He cuts the weeds by swinging a large wooden handled sickle, which leaves a large half circular pattern in the ditch. And while the five foot scythe is difficult to handle, Gene likes using it because it takes less time to clear out the weeds than when using the smaller hand sickle.

When there is no work assigned, it is especially enjoyable to lie on the cot on a rainy summer afternoon and listen to the rain hit the roof and trickle into the gutter. The rhythm provides background music for Gene as he reads.

He selects comics from the box under the cot. It is a community pool of comic books, and Jimmy, Vincent and Paul add and borrow comics from the box. The supply and kinds of comic books change weekly. The most popular are *Spiderman, Archie,* and *Superman;* but *Rubberman* is Gene's favorite. This character can stretch around buildings, squeeze under doors, and pull his body after him. There is no place Rubberman can't investigate, and there is no lack of corruption to fight even with the evil Japanese Empire and German Nazis defeated. Communism is now the evil power that must be stopped before it dominates the world and destroys America.

On the back cover of the comic books, Charles Atlas recommends his body building manual, so bullies will no longer kick beach sand in skinny boys' faces. And there are advertisements selling gag items like Joy Buzzers that you hide in your hand to surprise people when you shake their hand, and Whoopee Cushions that make strange unexpected noises when someone sits down on the cushion that is hidden in the seat of a chair. Gene isn't interested in gimmicks. He's looking for ways to make money.

He scans the ads looking for business opportunities and reads: *Raise Minks. It's Easy. It's Safe. It's Profitable.* This looks like a possibility since Gene already raises rabbits. Expanding into the mink business sounds like fun, and he will double his money in a year according to the advertisement. He completes the application and mails it. Within a few days the telephone rings, and Gene's dad answers the phone.

"Can I speak to Mr. Gene Millard?" asks the man making the call.

Gene's dad is suspicious of the caller. Gene never told his parents he sent in the inquiry.

"I'm Gene's dad. Can I help you?"

"I'm calling from Mink's International, and I would like to schedule a meeting when I can discuss the mink industry.

"There must be some mistake, Gene is twelve and busy with school and 4-H. He won't have time to start a mink farm."

After a brief explanation of Gene's financial situation, his dad hangs up and tells Gene, "I wish you had told me that you were considering starting a mink farm. This call surprised me, and I don't believe you have the money to start a farm."

"I was hoping I didn't need much money. I could use the rabbit cages and raise both rabbits and minks."

"They wanted several hundred dollars to begin with and an assurance you could provide furs every couple of months."

"Do you think they might take rabbit furs?"

"Gene, they deal in minks, not rabbits."

"I guess I can wait for a couple of years, but I'll keep looking for an opportunity to make money."

There was no more talk of raising minks, but Gene continues to scan the comic books for ways to make money. He spots an ad about becoming a taxidermist. There are lots of dead animals around the farm that he could practice on, so he sends in an application. His application to the mail order taxidermy school is accepted, and they request fifty dollars to be mailed to them before he can receive his first lesson. When the taxidermy school officials fail to receive their money, a marketing agent calls. Gene's dad answers the phone.

"Can I speak to Mr. Gene Millard?" asks the man on the other end of the phone.

Gene's dad thought he had made it clear that Gene wasn't interested in raising minks. Again the boy failed to tell his parents of his interest in mounting dead animals.

"I'm Gene's dad. Can I help you?"

"I'm calling from Mail Order Taxidermy School, and we haven't received the fifty dollars for the first lesson."

"There must be some mistake. Gene is busy with school and 4-H and doesn't have the time to learn the details of taxidermy, nor does he have the fifty dollars."

After a little more discussion about his son's ambitions, he hangs up and tells Gene, "I wish you had told me about your desire to become a taxidermist. This call surprised me."

"I thought I could practice on the dead animals around the farm."

"The dead farm animals can best be collected by the rendering works whose job it is to collect dead animals. And birds killed in a storm are dead way too long before you could stuff them. If you're still interested in four or five years you can look into becoming a taxidermist."

"I guess I was thinking too big," Gene replies disappointedly.

"It's okay to have big dreams, but they need to be realistic," his dad answers.

Gene's dreams of becoming a mink farmer or a taxidermist are shattered, but a new career possibility appears on the back of an *Archie* comic. He can apply for admission to an art school if he reproduces the drawing of a woman's face. He carefully sketches the face, completes the application, and mails it to the art school. Within ten days he receives a letter confirming that he has considerable drawing talent and is accepted into the art school. Unfortunately, the fifty dollar tuition is more money than he has saved.

Gene doesn't mail the fee, but this time there is no telephone call. His desire of becoming an artist joins the dead dreams of being a taxidermist or mink farmer. Nevertheless, he continues to scan the comic books for 'get rich schemes' disguised as career opportunities.

During the summer of 1948, Gene keeps busy in the Bristol Hawkeyes 4-H club, but he is tired of raising rabbits and won't be expanding into raising minks. He wants a project that is more adult. His dad is selling the milk cows, which are an international conglomerate of half breeds representing cows from different parts of the world. The herd consists of Jersey, Milking Shorthorn, Ayrshire, Holstein, and a breed that is not documented.

His dad wants to replace the entire herd with either Guernsey or Jersey cows. Gene helps his dad study the two different dairy breeds. Jerseys are good cream producers and have soulful eyes, but the Guernsey are known to produce more milk. The two breeds have the same fawnlike color; the Jerseys are a solid light brown and the Guernsey has white patches. Guernsey cows are larger than the Jerseys, and once their research is completed his dad buys seven Guernsey heifers. Gene adopts a Guernsey calf as his 4-H project.

He names the calf Cynthia after Elizabeth Taylor's role as *Cynthia* in the movie. Elizabeth Taylor probably would not be happy having a cow, even if it is a young calf, named after a character she played in a movie, but Gene is twelve and believes it is compliment to Elizabeth Taylor and the young girl in the movie.

Gene and the calf bond easily, and the calf follows him with a halter, obeys his directions, and is not easily frightened. The calf is entered into the Greene County Fair, and Cynthia wins a blue ribbon in the one-year-old category, a pretty impressive accomplishment for his first year in the dairy division.

Gene keeps Cynthia as his 4-H project for the following year and enters her as a two-year old heifer in the Greene County Fair. At the time of the fair, the two year old is nearly ready to give birth to her first calf, which is a disadvantage in the contest since she is overweight and has a sagging back. The judge starts by placing Cynthia and Gene at one end of the line of all the entries. Gene is bursting with pride and believes his calf is in first place. No. They are at the wrong end of the line. Cynthia places last and receives a third place white ribbon. Gene is told that his heifer is too close to delivery, and he should never have shown her at the county fair.

Gene could enter Cynthia and her calf into the cow and calf category as a third year project, but he fails to keep good records and decides to leave the dairy business. He sells the cow and calf back to his dad and decides to raise market pigs.

Many changes occurring on Iowa farms are much more important than Gene's decision to raise pigs. But some changes will make Gene's work easier, like cutting weeds along the farm ditches, a job that Gene detests. So when he reads that World War II chemists created herbicides that kill unwanted foliage he is excited about the findings. The newly discovered herbicides were used to destroy undergrowth in the jungles during the war, and are now available to kill the unwanted weeds in the road side ditches.

His dad is especially interested in the herbicides that will kill broad leaf plants, but not grasses like corn. Some farmers believe the chemicals might do more harm than good, and some believe the chemicals are too costly. For a while his continues to rely on the old fashioned way of keeping fields free of weeds: cultivate the corn early, at least three times, and remove the cockleburs and sunflowers using hoes and machetes. As for keeping the ditches weed-free; Gene's dads argues that as long as Gene can swing the scythe, there is no need to use the herbicides.

However, he may consider using herbicides to keep larger weeds from invading the corn. Keeping corn fields weed free is important because fields free of weeds provide more nourishment and moisture to the corn and result in higher crop yields, earning farmers more money. A field free of weeds is also easier to harvest, especially now that mechanical corn pickers have replaced picking corn by hand. Six foot cockleburs and sunflowers can plug up a corn picker and slow down the fall harvest, so the discovery of 2-4-D shows much possibility for keeping fields clean of weeds.

Neighboring farmers not using 2-4 D hire young boys and girls to cut cockleburs and sunflowers out of the corn. These young laborers also use hoes and corn knives to walk the beans and remove the noxious weeds from the bean fields that cultivating didn't remove earlier. One neighbor hires Gene to help him free the corn field of the noxious weeds.

Following the 1948 county fair Gene awakens before 6 am, carries water to the pigs and makes sure the pigs have corn to eat during the day. After breakfast he peddles his old bike a mile and half to the neighbor's farm to start work at 7am. The neighbor will pay him $1.00

an hour to hack cockleburs, velvet weeds, and sunflowers out of the corn field using large machetes.

Gene's long sleeved shirt and blue jeans become thoroughly soaked from the morning dew. The sharp corn leaves cut his face and neck, but the long sleeves protect his arms. The rawhide gloves protect his hands from getting blisters and cuts. The boy and the man work until noon, eat lunch, and take a rest before returning to work for another two hours. They avoid the afternoon heat in the hot cornfields and stop working at 3 pm.

By 3:30 Gene has returned to his home and is relaxing on the porch reading comics. Later in the afternoon he waters the pigs and helps milk the cows. After six days of working, the field is free of cockleburs, velvet weeds, and sunflowers and Gene earns his first paycheck of forty-two dollars.

"What you going to do with all your money?" Karla asks.

"I've got some ideas," Gene replies and thinks *I'm not taking her to a movie.*

It was difficult work, and Gene wants to buy something that he wants and not waste it on a girl. Since May he has been admiring a Columbia bicycle on display in the Jefferson hardware store. It features steel springs on the front wheel that absorb jolts when riding over rough spots. There is a headlight, powered by two batteries concealed in the panel between the crossbars. A companion's seat is attached above the rear fender. The bike is equipped with two wire saddlebag baskets straddling the rear wheel. The bike is a delight to look at and has everything but a horn.

The more costly Schwinn bicycle has a horn, but who needs a horn on farm roads? He wouldn't pass the cars that shared the gravel roads, and those riding on tractors couldn't hear a horn unless it was an air horn. With the earnings in his pocket, he buys the Columbia bicycle on a warm August Saturday evening. His dad packs the partially assembled bike into the family's 1941 Pontiac. He and his dad will assemble the bike the next day after attending church, eating Sunday dinner, and reading *The Sunday Des Moines Register*. It is late afternoon by the time the bike is assembled. *Who cares what time it is?* thinks Gene, The bike has a headlight, and I'm an experienced bike rider that knows how to ride at night. Gene checks the tires and looks for loose bolts. He is ready to take the bike on its maiden voyage.

"Don't ride too far," shouts his mom as Gene dashes out the lane and down the road hitting all the bumps he can to check out the shock springs. The stabilizing front springs make the bike handle better on the gravel road. Gene heads for Farlin and loses sight of how dark it is getting. About a mile from home he flips the light switch. The light blinks twice and goes out. No lights. He has no screw driver to remove the panel and inspect the batteries so he cautiously rides home in the near darkness.

His dad meets him as he enters the lane and asks, "Why is the light off?"

"I don't know. The batteries must have jiggled loose."

"Let's take a look."

Gene is right. The batteries are bouncing around in the encasement.

"The engineers designed the headlight for paved streets, not these rough roads," Gene tells his dad. From now on Gene never rides at night without making sure the batteries are not only clamped in but also tied in with some baling wire. For road emergencies, Gene keeps a small repair kit stored and tied to the wire saddlebag basket. The kit contains a small crescent wrench, screwdriver, black electrician tape and some baling wire. The kit along with the jack knife he carries keeps him from getting stranded on a trip to Farlin or Churdan.

When September arrives, Gene looks forward to returning to school. Art is gone; and Mrs. Williams actually makes school fun with music and art classes, interesting books to read, and projects. She understands that keeping him busy with projects keeps him from creating problems for himself or others.

"I've a special undertaking for those who are interested in creating a universe," announces Mrs. Williams the second week of school. "Who's interested?"

Immediately the three musketeers – Jimmy, Vincent, and Gene – raise their hands. Paul, sensing it might be a fun joins the three by raising his hand.

"You must complete your regular assignments first. But when you are done with your daily work, you can work on this project." She points to a large box on her desk that is labeled *Science Kit: Create a Universe for the Classroom.*

She tells the boys, "The instruction manual is on top of the box, and I'll leave it to you guys to create a universe."

There is much interest in outer space. The Germans had experimented with V-Rockets when attacking England and started using jetfighters at the end of the war. Russia and the United States are interested in developing their own rockets and perfecting jet airplanes.

Einstein's Theory of Relativity and his famous equation $E=MC^2$ is being discussed and reported in the newspapers because of the atomic bomb. Few people understand his theory or the equation, but many people understand that a new view of the universe is emerging. The new view of outer space is a far cry from the Flash Gordon comics or Jules Verne books written in the late 1800s.

This new endeavor is an excellent venture for the four boys. The Science Kit: *Create a Universe for the Classroom* is an exercise about the vastness of the universe and displays the earth as a very small piece of a much larger system. The accompanying manual explains that everything is moving in space and that there is no up or down.

"Gene, you're the oldest and the best reader. You read the instructions, and we will be the scientists to get the thing put together," volunteers Vincent.

"I can read," interjects Paul

"Yeah, me too," responds Jimmy.

"Let's draw straws as to who reads the manual," replies Paul.

Vincent pulls three straw stems from the broom in the storage closet.

"Whoever gets the long straw is the reader," offers Jimmy.

The three boys each draw a straw from Vincent. Paul pulls out the long straw.

"Okay short stuff. Read the instructions," speaks up Gene, somewhat disappointed that he isn't the reader and leader.

"It will take me some time to understand these instructions," reveals Paul. "I'll take it home and we can start tomorrow."

The next day after their daily assignments are completed the team begins working on the project. Different packets are taken from the box and laid on the floor in the back of the classroom. One is marked Earth and Planets, another is marked Sun and Moons, and a third marked Galaxy items. A small box holds clips, strings, and tape.

Paul instructs the others, "Start with the Earth and Planets packet."

Vincent, Jimmy and Gene begin assembling the planets which are made of heavy construction paper pieces that fold into spheres. The spheres are marked with names of the planets in the earth's solar system. The next day they assemble the sun, various moons, and they keep the assortment of balls in the rear of the classroom. After the pieces are assembled, they are hung from the ceiling.

The instructions suggest that they hang the earth's sun near the rear of the room and string the planets in their proper order around the sun. The moons are placed near the planets that have moons.

What is of special interest to Gene is that the earth's sun is not the center of the universe. It is only a star with planets revolving around it. The last phase of the project is assembling and hanging a variety of stars, comets, and other planet systems. There is a solar map in the kit, providing directions as to where to suspend them in various parts of the classroom. When the entire set of mobiles is completed, there is an array of stars and solar systems hanging from the classroom ceiling with our solar system occupying only a corner of the room.

The universe project keeps the four boys busy until Thanksgiving. They admire their work and are proud of their universe. All decide they will become scientists who study the universe. Gene learns that constructing a universe is way more fun than letting toads loose in the classroom as he and Jimmy did last fall.

Last summer Gene enjoyed swimming at the Jefferson municipal swimming pool and going skating in the town's skating rink with his new friends from 4-H, but he continues to enjoy movies. However, he is no longer devoted only to cowboy movies but has broadened his interest to include *Miracle on 34th Street, Life with Father, Bud Abbott and Lou Costello Meet Frankenstein,* and *I Remember Mama.*

There are Westerns that Gene enjoys like *Paleface,* which features Bob Hope and Roy Rogers singing "Buttons and Bows" to Jane Russell. He knows that the song was recorded earlier by Gene Autry and continues to believe it's unfair that Rogers gets the spotlight in too many movies. Gene harbors the belief that Autry is the better actor and cowboy, but Gene Autry is aging and cowboy movies are losing their appeal, not only to Gene but the public in general. Movies like *The Treasure of the Sierra Madre* and Western comedies like *Paleface* are replacing the older style cowboy movies.

After seeing *Paleface,* Gene walks around the barnyard singing "Buttons and Bows" as loudly as he can sing. Singing loud is something he learned from his dad who sings "My Red River Valley," "She Is My Sunshine" and "God Bless America" around the farm. And while his dad may not sound like Bing Crosby he can be heard a mile away on a quiet summer evening.

Gene's early teachers asked Gene to sing quietly, and Miss No Mistakes even requested him to mouth the words. By being told to sing quietly, he believes that he is not a very good singer and is surprised when Mrs. Williams asks him to sing "Hark the Herald Angels Sing" at the 1948 Christmas program.

Jimmy tells him, partly out of jealously, "You aren't such a good singer; you're loud."

"Maybe, but I'm going to take piano lessons and learn more about music than just singing," replies Gene. "Mrs. Williams told my mom and dad where they can buy an old upright piano. She thought it would be a good idea if I took piano lessons."

"Big deal," Jimmy answers. "I'm getting a guitar, and I'm going to start playing and singing and become famous like Roy Rogers."

"Okay, you play your guitar, but the cowboys are on their way out."

———

Cowboys and cowboy movies aren't the only things that are disappearing. There are fewer geese, ducks, and even pheasants. Gene's dad contributes the decrease in wild life to the draining of the marshy areas in the county and the farming of more land. He leaves a couple of rows of corn unpicked to provide food for pheasants. It isn't just because he is thoughtful, but he wants a few pheasant around to hunt in the fall.

Gene's mom enjoys decorating for Christmas, and the big luxury item for trees this year are the bubble lights. The lights are expensive, but the desire to have the newest fad is worth the price. The pent-up hunger to have something fun is strong after experiencing the 1930s economic depression and enduring the shortage of items during World War II. The family's house now has electricity, the farmland is productive, and the price for corn is good. And while they may not have plumbing or own their farm, they are willing to splurge on Christmas gifts this year. Gene's mother tells his dad on their way to Jefferson, "This year we are going to spend some money for Christmas – enough of going without."

When they climb out of the car, it seems that every window display is using bubbling Christmas tree lights. There is a moving Santa Claus

Where Did All the Cowboys Go?

with elves, waving to people from the Coast to Coast Hardware store. And decorated light poles around the square give the town square a holiday look that competes with the decorations in Fort Dodge or Des Moines.

"I'm going over to Ben Franklin's to price the bubble lights and buy some new tinsel for the Christmas tree."

"We'll meet you back here in an hour," answers Gene's dad.

His dad is looking for an electric mixer to give Gene's mom, and Gene tags along to look at the toys and games in the Coast to Coast Hardware. His dad examines the mixers and decides on the Sunbeam Mixmaster. It is no hand held mixer, but a large and practical mixer. It isn't as elegant as a Hamilton Beach or as stylish as the Dormeyer mixer, but it has its own bowl and the mixer moves up away from the bowl when not in use. The mixing blades can be lowered into the bowl; and the ingredients can be mixed on low, medium, or high.

"These new kitchen devices are a God-send for women as they mix up cakes or whip up potatoes," informs the store clerk as Gene's dad pays the clerk for the mixer.

"Can you gift wrap the mixer?" asks his dad

"Sure can."

"Good. We'll go over and look at your electric trains."

There are not only electric trains but also electric motors for Gilbert Erector Sets and even small electric stoves for girls, but it's the Gilbert Chemistry Set that excites Gene.

"Look at that chemistry set," Gene says as he studies the collection of bottles. "There must be at least twenty bottles of chemicals."

His dad reads several labels, "Aluminum sulfate, powdered iron, Borax......."

There are additional vials of dry chemicals shelved in the two panel metal case and a small alcohol-fueled burner stored beside several test tubes and tongs that can be used when heating experimentations.

"I bet I could make stink bombs, glues, and colored smoke bombs with this set."

There is also a larger three-panel chemistry set that includes a microscope and additional chemicals.

"Do you think you'd be happy with the smaller set?" asks his dad.

"Sure, and I promise not to make any stink bombs," laughs Gene.

"I'm not sure what we will be giving you for Christmas as there are so many things available," answers his dad as they leave the store.

This year's Christmas cedar tree is better shaped, and the new tinsel along with a string of mesmerizing bubbling Christmas lights improves the tree greatly from past Christmas trees. The bubbles burp from the base of the blubs which look like Christmas tree candles when Gene squints and blinks his eyes. On Christmas Eve, all of the gifts are unwrapped, but there is no chemistry set for Gene. He only receives some socks and handkerchiefs but as a seventh grader, he no longer hangs his sock for Santa Claus. Gene rationalizes, "Since I no longer believe in the old guy, I guess I don't get a big gift."

As they collect the wrapping paper, Gene's mom asks him, "Did you like your present? I knew you would guess what it was, so I hid it in the bedroom."

"I didn't get a gift from the bedroom," stutters Gene.

"We forgot. Oh my. We forgot." She hurries into the bedroom and returns with the two panel Gilbert Chemistry Set.

Immediately, Gene unlocks the metal case and begins reading the labels of the chemicals, "Zinc sulfate, tartaric acid, tannic acid, sulfur, strontium chloride, sodium thiosulfate. Gee whiz, this must contain every chemical known."

He continues to read the instructions book and examines the alcohol burner.

"Better stop reading and get ready for Midnight Mass," directs his mom. "And promise not to make any atomic bombs."

1949

Gene has fun with his new chemistry set throughout Christmas vacation. His mom isn't so sure it is such a wonderful gift since he creates a stink bomb that pierces everyone's nostrils and smells worse than the manure in the barnyard. Following the creation of the horrible odor, he ignites a smoke that penetrates and irritates his eyes as much as the nitrogen in the chicken house. The straw that breaks the camel's back is a yellow liquid that leaves stains on clothing, wood, or skin. The blotch on the kitchen table cloth is all his mother can take.

"Out," she shouts and ushers him through the back door into the cold.

"I'm experimenting. I'm an amateur," pleads Gene.

"If I want the house to smell like a barnyard, I'll bring the animals inside," replies his mom, giving him her notorious don't-do-it-again look.

The coal shed is no longer needed to store coal since the house is now heated by an oil burner. Gene sees the empty building as an opportunity and suggests, "When it warms up, I'll clean up the shed and use it as my lab. I'll be out of your way."

"Good, but for now, you're banned from making anything that stinks or stains."

Gene runs out of alcohol for the chemistry set's burner and goes searching for money in the bottom of his dresser to buy some alcohol. He discovers a comic book advertisement with the special garden seed offer.

He had saved the seed advertisement from the back of a comic book after his failed enrollment in the artist correspondence course. The ad guarantees the atomically treated seeds will produce extraordinary yields. The ad claims he can triple his money by selling the seeds for a dollar a packet or amaze his friends when they witness the giant plants in his garden.

He has worked in the family garden for years, assisted in picking vegetables, and knows how to preserve carrots for his rabbits. He is confident that he knows gardening and the "5+1 Bargain Packet" costs only three dollars. He will receive four packages of radishes, beets, peas, beans, and carrots, and a bonus package of pumpkins seeds. He can sell the twenty-one packets of seeds for one dollar making twenty-one dollars. Deducting the cost of three dollars will result in an eighteen dollar profit. That will be plenty for replenishing the chemicals for his chemistry set.

He sends for the garden seeds, waits for their arrival, and makes a list of possible customers: Mom, Aunt Daisy, and Jimmy's mother. This will be an easy way to make money, a lot easier than cutting sunflowers out of corn.

Gene returns to school on January 3 and brings his Gilbert Chemistry Set to put on display. His classmates stand around the table, anxiously waiting as Gene opens the metal case to reveal the contents. He cautions everyone to stay back as he handles the professional looking bottles and test tubes containing chemicals.

"Some of these are dangerous," he comments as he reads off the names: magnesium chloride, zinc sulfate, calcium chloride, sodium bicarbonate, and calcium carbonate. Holding up a test tube of his yellow staining concoction, he instructs them, "This is just an example of what can be made from this set when you are unsure of the chemicals you're mixing."

He pours some of the gooey fluid on a rag he brought and dares anyone to wash out the yellow stain.

"Big deal," comments Jimmy. "My dad has oil stains that Mom can't wash out. And lots of the stuff in that set can be found in a kitchen."

"But these are in purer forms, and some are chemical compounds only found in chemical labs. I made some really smelly stuff at home using these chemicals; they smelled so bad Mom kicked me outside," argues Gene.

"Is there any uranium in there?" asks Vincent.

"No, it's against the law to make atomic bombs," replies Gene, unaware of what the laws were regarding uranium.

"My Uncle Pete is leaving Iowa and going to Arizona to look for uranium. He's got a Geiger counter and everything," brags Vincent. Following World War II some men hoped to make their fortunes finding uranium, the product used in making atomic bombs; and there was hope that uranium mining might start another California gold rush.

"I think it is marvelous that Gene is going to be a scientist," interjects Karla. "He will be discovering new things; you just wait and see."

"My mom says only really smart kids become scientists," proposes Jenny.

"Gene ain't so smart. I've known him a long time," concludes Vincent. "My Uncle Pete is smart. When he discovers uranium, he will be very rich."

Vincent and Jenny debate as to who are smarter, scientists or miners.

"Scientists who work in lavatories are the smartest," defends Jimmy.

"Not lavatories, laboratories," instructs Jenny.

"What's the difference, anyway?" asks Vincent.

"Laboratories are where scientists work, and lavatories are toilets," Jenny explains.

"What's the difference? They both smell," laughs Jimmy.

The students laugh, and Mrs. Williams announces that it is time to begin studying.

The chemistry set is displayed on the table. Students going near the chemicals receive a repeat lecture from Gene about the dangers of the chemicals and how careful they must be when looking at the contents in the bottles. By Wednesday no one goes near the set or asks Gene any questions. On Thursday he takes the set home one day early. No one misses it.

The garden seeds arrive in early March – in a small box. Enclosed are the seed packets with the names of the seeds printed on very small envelopes. Gene's plan is to sell the seeds for a dollar a packet.

"You can't sell them for a dollar," explains his mom. "There are very few seeds in any of the envelopes."

"A dollar is the suggested price in the advertisement."

"Maybe for a quarter," his mom bargains.

"Fifty cents and no cheaper," argues Gene. "I've got to make some money."

"First, you have to get some customers. And I already have my seeds ordered from Earl May."

His Aunt Daisy agrees to buy the peas and beans for a dollar. Jimmy's mom buys the carrot, radish and beet seeds for a dollar. He suffers a dollar loss; but keeps the pumpkin seeds. Once the corn is planted and peeking through the ground, Gene plants the pumpkin seeds in the far end of the cornfield next to hills of corn. He then forgets them.

Earlier in the school year, Mr. Morris had distributed a list of songs that students are to practice and sing at the eighth grade graduation. The students are to rehearse the songs during the year and have them memorized by May. The students practice a great deal in April, and near the end of the month Mrs. Williams asks Gene to remain after school and practice, "God Bless America." She even encourages him to sing as loudly as possible even though there is no one listening.

The graduation day arrives, and over one hundred and twenty students from rural one-room schools meet in the Jefferson Methodist Church to practice for the eighth grade commencement. In the morning the fourth through seventh grade students practice singing for the eighth grade ceremony that is scheduled for 2 pm.

"Gene Millard, please come up here to the stage," announces the choir director.

Gene walks nervously down the aisle, up the steps to the stage and stands beside the director.

"Your teacher tells me you can sing, and I would like you to sing, God Bless America this afternoon. You'll have to sing loudly since there is no microphone."

"I can try," Gene replies as he looks somewhat frightened at all of the students in the audience.

"You can do better than try."

"I will."

Gene begins, but halfway through the song the director stops Gene and asks the students in the church, "Can you hear Gene in the back of the church?"

Several students shout out, "No."

"You must sing louder. Pretend there is a little old lady in the back of the church who can't hear you."

Gene replies politely, "That little old lady needs to move closer to the stage since there are lots of empty seats up front."

The students roar with laughter, and Gene loses some of his stage fright. He sings the song again, and the director is satisfied and requests that the students applaud his performance.

Neither Mrs. Williams nor Gene's mom approves of young people being too outspoken, but neither reprimands his comment. They believe children and adults should voice their beliefs, but in this situation Gene's motives were not noble and he was more interested in getting a laugh. The laughter did relax him, and in the afternoon he performs his first public solo in front of the parents, friends, and students at the eighth grade Greene County graduation exercise.

His willingness to sing before audiences becomes known and Gene sings such songs as "Danny Boy" and "Galway Bay" at the Catholic Church in Churdan. He also performs at farm bureau meetings singing popular songs like "Now Is the Hour," "A-You're Adorable," and in 1950 he performs "My Heart Cries for You" at a county wide event.

The freckled-faced, awkward, thirteen year old boy is invited to sing at a 1949 summer Farm Bureau meeting at the IOOF Hall in Farlin. Lately, his body parts grow in spurts, and his feet announce the arrival of his body before he enters the room. His lanky arms hang to his knees. He is tall and skinny with ears that stick out from under his reddish-brown hair. He enjoys singing and agrees to sing the popular song from Paleface, "Buttons and Bows." It is before the age of rock stars, and Gene is no Frank Sinatra, but there is a girl, Frieda who is waiting at the front door of the IOOF Hall when Gene goes outside after singing. She speaks softly from the shadows of the old building, "Hi Gene."

"Hi," Gene replies and sees Frieda standing under the elm tree. Gene met her at the Jefferson skating rink earlier this summer and saw her again at the graduation ceremony.

"How did you learn to sing like that?" she asks.

"I don't know. I just like to sing."

"Want to go for a walk?"

"Okay."

They walk toward the baseball field and talk about kids they know. Frieda is Karla's friend, and Karla has been friendlier to Gene since her older brother Art is no longer attending their school.

The evening is warm, and they sit on the ground, which still holds the sun's heat. She places her hand on Gene's knee and asks him, "Are you Karla's boyfriend?"

"No," chuckles Gene. She has never been his girlfriend, and he finds it amusing that someone would think she was.

"You going skating next Saturday?" asks Frieda. "If you are, we could meet at the rink."

Not aware of the entrapments that young girls are capable of, Gene agrees to meet her. She moves closer to Gene, and he is saved as people begin to leave the IOOF hall.

"I got to go back to the hall and meet my parents," Gene blurts out.

"See you Saturday," shouts Frieda.

Frieda's older sister sees the two leave the shadow of the building and giggles. "What have you two been doing?"

"Nothing, really, not a thing," protests Gene.

On Saturday night Gene skips his regular movie and meets Frieda at the skating rink. He skates with her a couple of times but devotes more time racing with John, a new friend he recently met at 4-H meetings. Karla is there and she and Frieda spend a great deal of time whispering and giggling as they skate to "The Tennessee Waltz."

John, Karla, Frieda, and Gene leave the rink at 9 pm to return to the town square to meet their parents and go home. Frieda suggests that they walk through the darkened city park on their way to the town square.

"It's out of our way," Gene protests and begins to the turn away from the park.

"Don't you like me?" pressures Frieda.

"Yeah," answers Gene.

"Well then, hold my hand and walk through the park with me." She grabs Gene's hand, and they walk together. The park is dark, and Gene urges the three to move along. He doesn't want his parents to see them or to be upset about his being late in meeting them.

Karla and John act silly, and Karla kisses John when they stop in the park. John doesn't object. Frieda pushes closer and closer to Gene and looks kind of funny.

"I've got to meet my parents."

"Meet me at the rink next week. I'm going to miss you, so please write me a note. Karla can give it to me in Farlin when she goes to church."

"Okay," Gene replies. All the way home he is quiet and wishes that he had not promised to write her a note or agree to meet her next week at the skating rink. But she is kind of exciting.

As a vulnerable seventh grader, Gene writes her a note taken from the song "A Tree in the Meadow." The note reads: *How can I forget you when you're always in my heart? You are with me every day and night or whenever we're apart.* Gene gives the note to Karla to deliver.

But as is often the case in clandestine relationships, things do not go as planned. Karla gives the note to Art to give Frieda's older sister since they both ride the same school bus. Frieda's older sister is to give it to Frieda, but Art, still upset about the bloody nose that Gene gave him, reads the note to the students on the bus. Gene's brother intercepts it from Art, but rather than give the note to Gene, his brother reads it to the family at supper. Gene is mortified. He doesn't write any more notes that he wouldn't share with his mother, and on the following Saturday he skips the roller rink and attends the movie *Abbot and Costello meet Frankenstein*. He isn't interested in kissing girls or holding hands, even if Frieda is exciting. Movies are more predictable.

Gene's experiences at Farlin and at the IOOF hall teach him valuable lessons that are not taught at Bristol 2. His mother's objection to the minstrel shows provides the groundwork for his learning not to be prejudiced toward a person of another color. His experience in the boxing ring was a not-so-gentle lesson in teaching him when to fight and when not to.

Charlie, who was generally covered with sweat and smoke, shows Gene the importance in hard and honest work. Gene knows that heating iron, bending steel, and flattening metal is an important service to the farmers in Bristol Township. And in the pool hall Charlie teaches him that the knowledge of playing pool is only part of the play. A good pool player can lose to a clumsy stranger who visits town to hustle the best player.

Not only does Gene learn to play eight ball in the pool hall be learns that men and women are not too different. On rainy days he watches farmers drop off cultivator and mower blades at the blacksmith shop to be sharpened and then escape to the pool hall to gossip. The men pass around rumors as easily as women do in a sewing circle.

The 4-H softball team plays their ball games in Farlin. Gene is not a good player and has never hit a home run. He always attends practices, is a team player, and never misses a game; but his physical coordination could be improved. He does learn that playing as a team member can be as important as having talent.

He also learns that the softball diamond is more than a ballpark; it's a communication center or at least a gossip hub. Spectators park their cars toward the ball diamond; so they can sit in the cars, watch the games, and visit with neighbors. They exchange rumors about who is dating whom and what married men or women are having affairs. They chitchat about who is moving out of state and what young men are leaving for the military service. They swap information that is never published in the *Jefferson Bee* or *Herald*.

Gene learns that he cannot judge people's motives by their behavior. Teenage girls watch the boys play softball and scheme ways to meet them after the games. Some practice diplomacy and talk to the boys, and some wait for the boys to come to them. Younger children play hide and seek around Farlin and report back to their parents every half hour. Some do so to assure the parents that they are safe; others, so that they won't get caught smoking.

He also learns something about communications and relationships at a box social in the IOOF hall. The Bristol Busy Bees Girls 4-H club sponsors a square dance followed by a box lunch. The girls pack lunches in fancy decorated boxes, and at the end of the dance the box lunches will be auctioned to the highest bidder. Gene is happy that neither Frieda nor Karla are members of the Bristol Busy Bees. If they were members one of them would be trying to persuade him to buy a lunch packed by the other.

After learning how to Allemande Left, Do Sa Do, and Circle Right, the young people promenade to the end of the hall where there is a table covered with colorfully wrapped red, blue, and green boxes, and two or three picnic baskets. The girls are seated on the left side of the hall, and the boys take seats on the right side.

A new girl whose parents recently returned from California tells John to tell Gene that her box is the blue one with the yellow ribbon. John whispers to Gene that the blue box belongs to the new girl with the brown eyes but fails to mention the yellow ribbon. When the biding starts; Gene's eyes are on a big blue box.

Holding up the large blue box and looking inside the auctioneer announces, "How much do I hear for this box?"

There are no bids.

He continues, "In here is freshly fried chicken, cold pop, and fresh apple pie. The apples were picked this afternoon. This pie is made by an experienced cook who knows how to make pies." The 'experienced cook' comment should warn most boys that it is a box made by an older woman, but the hint is too subtle for Gene.

"Who will give me fifty cents?"

There are no takers. Gene looks at John. John winks. The box is blue.

"Fifty cents," murmurs Gene.

"Who will give me a dollar?"

No bids.

"Sixty cents."

Silence in the hall.

"Sold to the young man for fifty cents."

The next box is the blue box with the yellow ribbon.

"How about fifty cents?"

"Here," yells John.

"A dollar, do I hear a dollar?"

"A dollar and quarter," shouts a young man in the back of the hall.

"How about two dollars?" continues the auctioneer.

"Two," yells John.

"Three, do I hear three."

"Three dollars," shouts the competitor from the rear of the hall.

"Three dollars and a quarter," barks John.

"Three fifty... Three fifty." Hearing no further bids, the auctioneer proclaims, "Sold to the determined boy in the yellow shirt."

Gene picks up the large blue box and looks for the girl who brought the lunch. It doesn't belong to a girl but to a spinster who is there to supervise the dance. John picks up the smaller blue box with the yellow ribbon and walks directly to the brown-eyed girl from California.

The older woman smiles and removes cloth napkins from the box and arranges the fried chicken, cold orange pop, small containers of baked beans, Jell-O salad, and two large pieces of apple pie on a table beside the napkins.

The pretty brown eyed girl unpacks the smaller blue box. There are to two egg salad sandwiches, dry-looking oatmeal cookies, and a small container of black olives.

The new girl, obviously wanting to be pampered, asks John, "Please get us two glasses of iced tea that the Bristol Busy Bees Girl's 4-H Club has provided."

Gene smiles at John and asks the older woman, "Were these apples really picked this afternoon?"

Gene arrives at school early on Monday, September 5, 1949, and inhales the smell of freshly mowed bluegrass, foxtail, and clover. He is entering the eighth grade, which will be his last year attending a rural school. After he successfully completes the eighth grade and passes the Iowa Eighth Grade Examination, he will attend the high school in Jefferson, Iowa.

There are changes in the one room school building since he began in 1941. The community water pail has been replaced with a large blue porcelain crock fountain that dispenses water using a bubble apparatus. There is a small electric hot plate that is used to heat the noon meals delivered by the mothers. Electric light bulbs hang from the ceiling, and the large potbelly coal/wood burning stove has been replaced with an oil burning heating stove. The teacher no longer needs to arrive early in the winter to stoke the coal. The oil heater's thermostat is set on low when leaving the school and is turned up in the morning.

The large globe that once occupied a stand has been replaced with a smaller globe that sits on a library table in the rear of the classroom, and the school is developing a small library, which includes more than two sets of encyclopedias.

Mrs. Williams is busy at her desk checking the list of students who will be attending Bristol 2 when Gene enters the classroom.

"Good morning, Gene."

"Good morning."

"Are you ready for another year?"

"Yes, and this year I'll need to get ready for high school. My oldest brother graduated last year and is planning to work in Des Moines. He says that the four years in high school really go fast."

"Time goes fast when we're busy, and I've got a project that you may be interested in."

"Yeah?" Gene answers with some hesitation.

"Mr. Morris provided all the rural school teachers with a list of students from other countries that are interested in writing to students in the United States. They are looking for pen pals. Do you think you'd be interested?"

Gene looks over the list and selects three students to write to.

>Gisela Winnaer
>Wiesentr 28
>Hamburg 19, Germany
>
>Diana Liu
>P.O. Box 140
>Kohala, Hawaii
>
>Eduardo S. V. Marfori
>Tagbilauau Bohol,
>Philippines

He writes a letter to each of the students telling them he is thirteen years old, five foot ten inches tall, weights one hundred and twenty-nine pounds, and has reddish-brown hair. He explains that he lives on a farm and that they grow corn, soybeans, hay, and oats. He describes the small Guernsey herd of twelve milk cows and the seventy-five or so chickens they keep to produce eggs. He introduces his three brothers and explains that one has graduated from high school, one is in high school, and one attends the rural one-room school with him.

Gene doesn't receive a reply from either Gisela or Diana although he was hoping to correspond with Gisela, so he could learn more about Germany by writing to a real German. The war had painted a very negative picture of the Germans, and he has German relatives who are nice. He hoped that Gisela could help him better understand more about Germany and its people.

Early in October Gene receives a reply from Eduardo.

> Eduardo S.V. Marfori
> Tagbilarau, Bohol, Philippines
> September 30, 1949

Dear Gene,

    I was so glad to receive your letter from Iowa. I hope your writing me don't bother you. Before I begin my errors are under care.

    I am already 14. I was 14 last January 23. By nick name is Eddie. I am only 5ft tall. I have black hair and eyes and my complexion is tan. I am a senior in high school I will graduate from high this March 1950. I am planning to take more classes after graduation. I hope my grade and age don't keep you from writing me.

    I go to the Holy Naivety College, a catholic school for boys and girls. It is directly by the SVD father. It has 3 departments. Elementary, High School and

College. What Church do you belong? I hope you'll tell me.

The hobbies are all sort of collections, such as stamps, shells, picture postcards, movie start photos, matchboxes, campaign pins, broaches, rings, Bird photos, leaves and flowers, novels, and mystery books comics. I also like to dance, sing, bike, swim, hike, baseball, and play the piano. I hope you'll send me anything that will add to my collections, send me your picture too.

My pop and mom are still living. My pop is a Liseal. My mom does the housework. I have 3 older sisters; Einwa 21, Linda 17, Tess 16 and older brother 20. They are all in College. I have 2 younger brothers and sisters. They are in fourth grade except Joe who is 2.

I have a pet dog, he is half police dog and have native. His name is Pirmee. I also have a pet cat whose name is Kitty.

Well, I can't tell you now about where I live, but I promise to tell you next time. I have to answer 29 letters more.

Lastly, I'm sending my best regards to your pa, ma, your brothers and hope the best for you.

May god bless you.

                Your new pal
                Eddie

P.S. Answer soon!

"When are you going to harvest the pumpkins in the back forty?" asks Gene's dad after surveying the forty acres on the far southwest end of the farm.

"Oh my, gosh, I forgot about my atomically treated pumpkins seeds."

His dad replies, "I don't know if there is anything atomic about them. They weren't glowing when I saw them, but there are a lot of them. You better take a wagon with you when you go to bring them in."

Gene pulls the small wagon, which is used around the farm, to the pumpkin patch and discovers over fifty pumpkins. Not the small pie pumpkins, but the fifteen to twenty pound jack-o-lantern hybrids. These big guys are not good for making pies, but they are great for making jack-o-lanterns. Stacking five or six pumpkins on the wagon each trip, he harvests all of them in ten trips. He unloads and stacks them next to the garage. There are quite a few. Maybe there is something special about the seeds, but Jimmy's mother and his Aunt Daisy never said anything about the vegetable seeds they bought. He is left not knowing if they are special or not.

He keeps four pumpkins for making jack-o-lanterns and his mom attempts to make a pie from one of them. The pie taste nasty. The pulp is stringy and flavorless and not like the sweet smooth textured pies made from the small mellow pie pumpkins. He can't sell them for making pies, or he will lose any credibility he might have.

"The best thing you can do is give them away," advises his dad.

Gene carts twelve pumpkins to school and offers a free pumpkin to any student in Bristol 2. Mrs. Williams turns the gift into an art lesson. As an art project, she invites students to draw a scary or funny jack-o-lantern face, which can be made into a template. Students can take the template home along with the pumpkin. Gene doesn't know how many students participate in the art project, but the pumpkins disappear. He also informs his relatives that they can help themselves to the pumpkins stacked next to the garage. After the first freeze, only a few wrinkled pumpkins are left.

His success as an entrepreneur is mixed. He never became a taxidermist or mink rancher, and art school was ruled out. Selling atomically energized seeds failed, but he is successful at growing pumpkins. Maybe success isn't always measured by how much money is made and that the journey may be more interesting than the goal. So he continues to survey comic book advertisements for opportunities to go into business.

He doesn't discover a business opportunity but reads an advertisement that entices him to join a book club. He sends in his membership fee of three dollars plus another dollar for a skull candleholder. Within the month a very small candleholder and four mimeograph short stories arrive in the mail. The stories are not about Huck Finn, Heidi or the March sisters in *Little Women*. Two of the stories are harmless detective stories taking place on the Mexican/Texas border, and the third story is about a dead man that returns from another world to assault his wife.

It is the fourth story that Gene reads several times. It is about a striptease dancer's capabilities that a thirteen year old boy knows nothing about. He reads the story, rereads it, and decides he doesn't know enough about females to understand it fully. He places all four of the stories in the community comic book box. He returns to the box to retrieve the stories with hopes that he can reread the one about the stripper and share it with Jimmy.

His mom may have confiscated the stories and destroyed them, or maybe his older brother found them and is saving them for his own reading. In any case, he doesn't report the theft; he knows he would have to explain the stories and that would be embarrassing. He doesn't want to receive a lecture from his mom. Telling Father Murphy at confession on Saturday night will take care of his guilt. After all, a priest won't know any more about women than he does.

Gene's only sister is born in November, 1949, a couple of weeks before Thanksgiving. His mom spends over ten days in the hospital; maybe to give her some relief from a house full of men, or maybe to give her a reason for not preparing a large Thanksgiving meal. Nevertheless, Gene is happy that he has a baby sister and enjoys watching her learn to crawl and climb on furniture. She will grow up in a family that is different from the family in which he is raised mainly because the economic environment has improved. The family is not wealthy, but corn prices are higher and conditions in Iowa have changed for the better. There is now electricity, better farming techniques, improved corn and soybean seeds, effective county extension services, and more opportunities for rural people to participate in the community. His parents will maintain the same value system and expectations for his sister that they did their four sons, even though she is the only baby boomer born into the family.

This year more attention is directed toward his new sister than the holiday activities. Nevertheless, Thanksgiving and Christmas are celebrated in the usual manner. Thanksgiving dinner is celebrated at his Aunt Leona's home, his uncles go pheasant hunting with his dad and brothers, and the family goes to Midnight Mass on Christmas Eve.

The week before Christmas Mrs. Williams reads the first few pages from the *Christmas Carol* to the students. She doesn't finish the story, and when the students leave for Christmas vacation she loans the Charles Dickens's novel to Gene.

During vacation he reads about Ebenezer Scrooge and tries to visualize the three Christmas ghosts, particularly Christmas Present who lives for only one day. In one section the ghost of Christmas Present reveals the shabby boy Ignorance and the starving girl Want. The ghost warns Scrooge to be especially frightened of the boy. The visualization of Ignorance remains with Gene. The impact is probably because Gene's dad has often reminded him that the lack of knowledge is the cause for many problems, and he encourages Gene to read and learn as much as possible.

Nevertheless, reading can become tiresome, and Gene enjoys taking a break and listening to the radio programs: *Fibber Magee and Molly, Jack Benny, The Grand Ole Opry,* and *The Shadow*. And on Sunday afternoon, Christmas vacation or not, it is especially enjoyable to eat popcorn covered with hot fudge candy, turn on the radio, and hear "Who knows what evil lurks in the minds of men?"

This Christmas vacation Gene attends the movie *Little Women*; a film that boys are not expected to enjoy. Although Gene enjoys the movie as much as he enjoyed reading the book. However, he doesn't share his interest in the movie or his junior high crush on Elizabeth Taylor, who plays Amy in the Hollywood version of the March girls' story.

However, he is more vocal about his admiration for Gene Autry who releases a new song, "Rudolph the Red-nosed Reindeer" which becomes the number one record in 1949, and is one of the all-time favorite songs for the remainder of the twentieth century. And although his interest in cowboys has declined, Gene enjoys reminding his dad and Jimmy that he remains a Gene Autry fan.

1950

"I hope the next fifty years will be better than the last fifty," Gene's dad says softly as he folds the January 1, 1950, Sunday issue of *The Des Moines Register* and lays it on the red Formica kitchen table. "We've had two world wars, a major depression, and the creation of weapons that are inconceivable."

"The world isn't getting better," replies Gene. "The Communists have taken over China, and there's trouble in North Korea."

"The world can be a pretty scary place. But we have electricity, and farming is getting easier. The discoveries of herbicides and pesticides have made living on the farms easier. And they are using plastics and new material to improve most everything – just look at this Formica on this chrome table."

Changes can be seen everywhere: there are fewer deer and pheasants, the road sides have fewer weeds, and electric lights can be seen throughout the countryside. Gene no longer plays outdoors in an imaginary land or pretends he is in a country of his own making. He and his dad no longer follow the ritual of attending a Saturday Western movie, but Gene hasn't forgotten Gene Autry.

Throughout the Christmas season, Gene Autry is singing, "Rudolph the Red-nosed Reindeer" or his earlier song, "Here Comes Santa Claus" almost every day on the radio. And when the movie *Riders in the Sky* comes to the Howard Theater during his vacation, Gene goes to see his childhood cowboy hero and listens to him sing "Ghost Riders in the Sky." The movie isn't very good and Frankie Lane's recording of Ghost Riders becomes a much more popular recording.

His disappointment in *Riders in the Sky* persuades Gene to watch different Western movies like *Red River* and *She Wore a Yellow Ribbon* starring John Wayne. John Wayne and Henry Fonda pair up to make a good Western in *Fort Apache*. Even the tough guy, Humphrey Bogart, from the old detective movies is excellent in *The Treasure of the Sierra Madre*. Gene's interest in the West is changing. Maybe that is why he sends for his first issue of the magazine, *The Open Road for Boys*.

The first issue includes stories about the Kodiak Bears in Alaska, and tales of men surviving snow storms in the Rocky Mountains. On the back cover of the magazine is an application to join the Open Road Pioneer's Club, a club designed for boys. He submits an application and waits for a reply. Within a week he receives his membership certificate signed by Deep River Jim, the Campfire Chief; a badge; and a membership pin.

As a member, he learns to identify and classify various birds and how to build and start a campfire. There are instructions for identifying constellations if he were to be lost in a forest. Gene soon earns the Trailsman feather pin and begins works to earn the rank of a Woodsman. He sets a goal to become a Hunter and eventually an Explorer. The magazine costs ten cents a copy, and in addition to the adventure stories there are cartoon contests. Gene draws several of the cartoons, but never mails them in. The club keeps him interested in the outdoors.

When Gene completes the eighth grade at Bristol 2, he can attend high school in Churdan or Jefferson, but he and his parents decide it is best if he attends the Jefferson High School that his brothers attended. His mom and dad are pleased with the education of his two older brothers, and the expense of a high school education is not a problem since the

Bristol Township pays for his tuition and transportation to the high school. Earlier in the 1940s it was the parents' responsibility to transport the student to the school even though the tuition was paid for by the township. In 1945 when his oldest brother started high school, his brother had to ride his bike a mile and wait to catch a ride to Jefferson High. Following the end of World War II, the school districts began to provide transportation for those living over two miles from the high school. Gene, along with numerous rural students, benefit from this new service.

Gene's mom attended a rural school prior to her attending Jefferson High and believes it will benefit him if he visits the high school before starting in September. She arranges a visit in hopes that Gene can meet some of the teachers. He climbs aboard the school bus on an overcast April morning in 1950 to visit classes, meet teachers, and encounter students.

The bus doesn't go directly to the high school but picks up students throughout Bristol Township as they wait by their mailboxes. The roadside looks different than it did nine years ago when he started school. Chemical herbicides have killed the wild strawberries and poison ivy that filled the ditches. Electrical wires are strung from pole to pole, carrying electricity to farmsteads. There are no wild plum bushes or small mulberry trees growing along the side of the road, and no milkweeds for Monarchs to feed or lay their eggs. Wild hemp and cattails no longer hide pheasant nests. The marshes have disappeared and been replaced by long rows of corn.

The bus stops at the west side of the three story high school building, and students scramble out the door. "The bus will leave here at 4:05. Be sure you're here," reminds the bus driver.

"How will I know which bus?"

"It's bus number 7. Or look for me, I'll be the driver," replies the portly, good natured man.

Gene enters the building and is met by students hurrying to their lockers and rushing off to classes. Gene looks at the schedule that has been prepared for him by the school principal.

Algebra – room 201, General Science – room 302, study hall, lunch hour, English 9 – room 212, industrial arts – room 104, study hall.

"Where's room 201?" Gene asks a man who is holding a broom.

"Up the stairs, and it's the first room on the right."

As Gene begins to leave, the man adds, "Remember you go up the stairs on the west end of the building and down the stairs on the east end."

"Thanks." Gene hadn't thought of traffic control.

The algebra teacher is friendly and introduces him as a guest and future student. When leaving the classroom, two girls approach him, and the prettiest one asks, "You're new, aren't you?"

Gene squirms and answers, "Yeah. I'm visiting."

"Which class are you headed for now?" asks the girl who is wearing a tight sweater.

Gene notices the sweater and begins to blush. "Science" is his one-word response.

"Up the west stairs and to your left," both girls respond. They walk away giggling and turn to make sure he is headed in the right direction.

In the general science class, Gene enters into the class discussion and explains how pulleys work when putting up hay in a hayloft. He impresses the teacher, who makes a point of saying that he looks forward to having Gene in class next year. Some of the students see him as tall lanky country geek, and others only wonder why he said anything at all.

Returning from lunch, the two girls, he met earlier, greet him and ask how his day is going. They flirt, and Gene remains quiet while his ears turn slightly red.

Gene has learned about pulleys, the basics of electricity, and go-carts powered by old washing machines engines by living on a farm, which is a natural environment to learn basic sciences. He also knows about the birthing of piglets, and the principles of plant growth. Science class should be easy, but his knowledge of science doesn't help him talk with girls. During the upcoming high school years he will decide if girls or pulleys are more interesting.

During April of 1950 Gene prepares for the Iowa Eighth Grade Examination. For ninety years, Iowa students attending one-room county schools have been required to pass the state exam before being admitted to a city high school. Gene and twenty-two other students from Greene County will be required to pass the test in order to attend a high school in the county

Mrs. Williams has explained to him that he must be able to read at the eighth grade level, and solve arithmetic problems to make certain he is ready for algebra. He must also understand the fundamentals of grammar, social studies, science, health, and music. Mrs. Williams provides past eighth grade tests for Gene to review. She tells him, "The questions won't be the same, but they will be similar."

"Can I take the test home?"

"No, this isn't used to memorize the test questions. It is to give you an idea of what the test looks like and the areas in which you will be tested."

Gene reviews the test for an afternoon and returns it to Mrs. William's desk. He is now aware there will probably be over five hundred questions and it will take all day to complete.

He is comfortable in being tested on reading, and while he won't answer questions over the books that he has read the reading examples in the tests don't appear difficult. And He notices that the reading areas included newspaper stories and radio scripts.

The earlier state arithmetic test assessed the ability to do mathematic computations and to know the meaning of terms like area, line, and the hypotenuse of a right triangle. Overall he believes the arithmetic tests look easy. The past vocabulary words look difficult, and he studies all kinds of vocabulary words including constitutional amendment, embargo, drought, allies, rebates, statute, nutrition, scientific theory, bacteria, quarantine, and interdependent. Mrs. Williams encourages him to study health topics like immunization, tooth decay, how diseases are spread, and even how to read an electric meter.

Neither Mrs. Williams nor Gene worries about the music test. He plays the piano so knows the difference between the treble and bass staff, the different values of the notes, and the names of the songs the students have been practicing during the year.

Gene enjoys history and current events. He has been reading *The Des Moines Register* since the beginning of World War II. From his interest in the news he learns what countries are communist, which countries are revolting, and where they are on a world map. He still plays, "name the country game" that he created using a globe when he began school, but he now uses a world atlas. From the newspaper he learns of treaties that the United States signs, why labor unions sometime strike, and of the troubles in the country of North Korea.

Gene joins twenty-three eighth grade students. Nineteen are from one-room schools in Bristol, Grant, Greenbrier, Highland, Jackson, and Willow townships, and four are from St. Mary's, a parochial school located in Grand Junction, Iowa. They will take the eighth grade test on May 15, 1950. The County School Superintendent and his assistant will administer the day-long examination in the Greene County Court House.

Four days later on May 19, 1950, Jessie M. Parker, State Superintendent of Public Instruction, addresses the students and presents eighth grade diplomas to the students. Gene and two other students are recognized as Honor I Students for having done exceptionally well on the test, and for their overall eighth grade academic achievement. All of the students completed the exam; however, not all go to high school. Some stay on the farm and others may not have scores high enough to be admitted to a city school.

On Monday May 22, 1950, Gene returns to the one-room school to pick up his books and say goodbye to Mrs. Williams and the students who will be retuning next fall. The students gather around and wish him success at high school. Gene also gives a letter to Mrs. Williams to mail to his pen pal in the Philippines.

> Jefferson, Iowa
> May 20, 1950

Hello Eddie:

    I better sit down and write to you now. I have been very busy this spring. We have all our crops in now. All of our oats are up good, and the beans and corn are coming up also. I am very sorry that I could not make you a snow man. But after I received your letter we got only one more blizzard and a few small snows. The blizzard was too dirty. The other snows were too small to make a snow man. You asked me if I had a girl. I don't and I am not starting now. Where do you get it that you're the funniest looking and ugliest person? I think that you are very handsome indeed; you asked me if it got cold here in the winter. It surely does. The coldest it got last winter was about 30 below zero and that was pretty cold. What is the average temperature there? The first part of this spring has been warm and rainy. We got 2 1/5 in. rain here last night. We have had an addition to the family, a girl Karen. They had a state test for the 8th grade students May 5, 1950. The graduation was May 19th. I was the high student for Greene County. My grades were: Literature A, Music A+, Daily average A. State test A, Average over everything A. I am ready for high school now.

    I have joined another club called the "Open Road Pioneer's Club." It is like Boy Scouts. Do you belong to Boy Scouts?

I am enclosing some picture of what the snow is like here in Iowa. The car is my brother's car in the picture. Signing off.

God Bless You.

                Your pal,
                Gene Millard
                Jefferson, Iowa USA

P.S. I also smashed my finger the other day. Here are some girls I write to:
Gisela Winnaer
Wiesentr 28
Hambury 19, Germany

Diana Liu
P.O. Box 140
Kohalam Hawaii
P.S. 2 if this is not what you wanted, tell me so.

Gene and Eddie do not exchange additional letters. Both will be busy with the challenges of becoming men.

When Gene leaves the school Jimmy is sitting on the steps waiting for him. Jimmy stands up and gives his buddy a punch in the shoulder, "We'll be fishing this summer. No reason to say goodbye."

"Yeah, we got a lot of fishing to do, but for now I have to help Dad plant corn."

Corn is planted using a two-row, horse-drawn planter. A wire extends from one end of the field to the other. There is a wire knot every forty inches which causes the planter to release three or four kernels into a small furrow created by the planter. Planting takes two people. One drives the team of horses across the field with the planter, and the other person moves the checkrow wire forty inches when the horses reach the other end of the field. At the other end, the driver gets off the planter and moves the checkrow wire forty inches in the same direction, assuring that the wire is straight with the other end. This procedure creates a "near perfect" pattern of corn hills with corn planted every forty inches. No matter how someone looks at the corn field, the rows are aligned.

The practical advantage is that the corn can be cultivated both lengthwise and crossways and finally "laid by" on the third plowing. After the three cultivations, the field won't be visited until harvest time unless there is a difficult patch of cockleburs or sunflowers that escaped the cultivator and need to be removed by hoeing or chopping them out with a corn knife.

Clickety-click Clickety-click Clickety-click the sound of the planter dropping kernels of corn into the Iowa soil fades as Gene's dad rides the horse-drawn planter across the black earth. Gene is there to move the checkrow wire.

A seldom-mentioned reason for the meticulous planting pattern is that a farmer's character may be judged by how straight the corn rows look lengthwise, crossways, and diagonally. There are similarities between the carefully planted corn field and Gene's completion of grade school. His nine years of schooling is to develop qualities that are admired from any view. And his reputation might well reflect the character of those who nurtured and cultivated him.

―――

That evening Joe McCarthy, a senator from Wisconsin, is ranting over the radio about the dangers of Communism and the USSR. Gene and his dad listen to the Senator attack those he believes are disloyal to the United States.

Gene interrupts, "It seems like the Soviet Union is causing lots of problems spreading Communism. Do you think that they might attack us?"

"Probably not, but maybe we should have been harder on them at the end of the war," answers his dad.

"What could we have done?"

"I suppose the Allies could have told Stalin we wouldn't stand for dividing Germany and Korea. But there is no reason in war, only in the causes of war."

"Do you think we will go to war again?"

"No," his Dad answers quickly, too quickly to satisfy a fourteen year old boy.

McCarthy rants on.

North Korea invades South Korea on June 25, 1950. President Truman orders a police action using ground forces on June 30, 1950. Some of the returning World War II veterans at the Farlin pool hall say Korea will be the last battle of World War II. The tall thin boy questions if wars will ever stop.

Meanwhile Gene stuffs memories of World War II and those of his cowboy heroes into the back of his mind. High school starts in September.

Epilogue

As children, we run where freedom exists, fight wars where battles are always won, and learn more than we are taught. As we age, our memories like an August morning fog or a January blizzard disfigures reality and cloud the memories we cherish, but the people continue to live in our thoughts.

Mrs. Williams, the wonderful teacher during my middle school years continued to teach at Bristol 2 until 1959, when the one room school was closed. She continued her teaching in the Churdan Public Schools, Churdan, Iowa, until her retirement. Her daughter, Mrs. Betty Reese, and her two granddaughters, Mrs. Linda Minnehan and Mrs. Nancy Croy also became Iowa teachers. Mrs. Reese and Mrs. Minnehan retired from teaching, and Mrs. Croy continues to work as an elementary principal in Wisconsin.

Bristol 7, where Gene began school, is a historical museum on the Greene County Fair Grounds in Jefferson, Iowa, serving as a memorial to one room schools in Greene County. Bristol 2 is believed to have been sold to a local farmer but no longer exists except in the memories of those who attended the school.

Jimmy died in 1982 at the age of 45. After graduating from Bristol 7 he attended the Churdan High School in Churdan, Iowa, and then served in the United States Army. Much of his life he lived in Texas getting closer to the real cowboys than Gene ever did.

Very little remains in Farlin that Gene would recognize, the IOOF hall is gone, the two churches have disappeared, the two room school has been torn down, and there is no post office, pool hall, or blacksmith. The railroad no longer disturbs the community because there are no railroad tracks, and the softball fields now produce corn.

The only buildings left in Farlin are a couple of homes and the grain elevator that is collapsed, and it would serve as a challenging setting for Gene and Jimmy to reenact a shootout, or overpower a German stronghold.

The Hardin creek still floods, but there are fewer trees and shrubs, and the farm land appears much closer to the water than when the two boys swam and fished in the muddy water. There are no farm buildings left on either of the farms where Gene lived and the small marsh that served as Gene's science laboratory has disappeared along with the Howard Theater where he watched Gene Autry and Hopalong Cassidy on Saturday afternoons. The Sierra Theater has replaced the Iowa Theater. The statue of Abraham Lincoln remains on the Greene County Courtyard grounds standing guard over the old Lincoln Highway which was also Highway 30, however Highway 30 is now north of the town. The County Court House still serves the county, but there is no County School Superintendent's office since all of the one-room schools are gone

Changes continue to emerge to meet new needs in Bristol Township and Greene County, which is the way it should be. There is a new generation that is creating their own memories, and at some point they will likely reflect back on their youth and ask: where did all their cowboys go?

About The Author

Joe Millard graduated from Bristol 2 in Greene County, Iowa and then attended High School in Jefferson, Iowa. After high school he attended the University of Iowa in Iowa City, Iowa for a year and one semester. He then served two years in the United States Navy aboard the USS Yorktown to complete his military obligation. Following his discharge from the United States Navy he attended Iowa State Teachers College in Cedar Falls, Iowa. In 1960 he received a Bachelor of Arts Degree in Social Science with an emphasis in History and in 1964 a Master of Arts degree in Secondary School Administration. Following his experience as a high school principal Joe returned to college at Iowa State University in Ames, Iowa and was granted a PhD in Education in 1970.

He taught American History, American Problems, and mathematics in the Urbana and Postville, Iowa public schools, and then served as the High School Principal in Story City, Iowa, and at Wahlert High School in Dubuque, Iowa. Dr. Millard retired in 1996 as the Director of Education for the Heartland Area Education Agency in Johnston, Iowa, having worked there for 25 years. He has taught undergraduate courses at Iowa State University, Ames, Iowa, Drake University, Des Moines, Iowa, and the Des Moines Area Community College in Ankeny, Iowa. Joe has been published in educational periodicals, story magazines, poetry publications, and research journals. He and his wife are retired and live in Waukee, Iowa, and currently they travel throughout the United States visiting their children and grandchildren.

Where Did All The Cowboys Go? is Joe's second published memoir. His first published book, *The Quiet Journey,* is a collection of memoirs that was published in 2007. He also published a book of poems in 2003 titled, *Seeing Though Gray Colored Lens*. In retirement Joe enjoys writing and talking with groups about writing their memoirs.

Dr. Millard believes history should not be confined to academic books or locked up in the archives, but made personal by individual stories. These narratives, when told by persons who have lived ordinary lives, reveal an authenticity that is left out of history books.

Reading Club Discussion Questions

In your youth did you have the fondness for outdoor activities as much as Gene?

Why do you believe Mrs. Frohling is quiet about the bombing of Pearl Harbor?

Did you every have a movie star hero like Gene Autry or a crush on a movie starlet like Elizabeth Taylor?

Were you ever impacted by a war?

What are the reasons that Jimmy and Gene become good friends?

Did you have a close friend growing up?

Discuss ways in which the one room schools may have failed to meet Gene's needs.

Discuss ways in which the one room school system may have met Gene's needs.

What community events that Gene participated in would be unacceptable today? Did you participate in any activities that promoted discrimination or bullying?

As a youth did you have a bully to contend with?

Did you have a teacher that me your needs at a time when you needed him or her?

Were you required to pass an eighth grade examination or a test before being promoted to the next grade? Is testing a good idea for promoting students?

Major changes in public health and medical practices occurred during the 1940s. What health practices are changing today?

Do the questions in the State Eighth Grade Tests in "Appendix A" look similar to the test questions that you took in eighth grade? Which of the tests do you find most interesting?

Discussion questions for young readers

Why does Gene appear to have such a fondness of the milkweeds, cattails, monarch butterflies and the outdoors in general?

Gene's hero is Gene Autry. Who are the heroes today?

Why do you believe Mrs. Frohling is quiet about the bombing of Pearl Harbor?

How is Gene impacted by World War II?

What are the reasons that Jimmy and Gene become good friends?

Discuss ways in which the one room schools may have failed to meet Gene's needs.

Discuss ways in which the one room school system may have met Gene's needs.

Why were movies and books so important to Gene? Are they that important today?

What community events that Gene participated in would be unacceptable today?

What did Gene prove in the fight with Art?

What did Mrs. Williams do as teacher that made Gene a better student?

Why was the State Eighth Grade Examination so important and is testing that important today?

What changes in public health and in the medical practices improved the overall health of citizens in the 1940s?

Does the State Eighth Grade Tests in "Appendix A" look more difficult or easier than the tests you take today?

Student Activities

Listed are student activities that will help them become more aware of life during the1940s?

1. Research and write a report about a World War II home front project. Topics could be any of the three topics listed below, or another activity related to the home front during World War II.
    a. World War II Saving Bonds and the posters used to sell the bonds.
    b. Scrap drives for iron, rubber, or even kitchen grease that was collected for the war effort.
    c. The rationing of food and items needed for the war effort.

2. Research and write a report on the changes that took place following World War II. Topics might include:
    a. The impact that the draining of the marshes in the Great Plains or Midwest had on the future.
    b. The ramifications of using herbicides or insecticides

3. Prepare questions to ask someone who was alive in the 1940s. Invite the person to the classroom to answer your questions. Or arrange an interview with the person in his or her home.

4. Do not use your cell phone, texting, or email from nine in the morning until three in the afternoon. Make a list of how your communication patterns are different than those of students in the 1940s.

5. During World War II the Nazis exhibited a horrendous hatred toward Jews and killed many innocent people. Following the attack on Pearl Harbor the United States Government created special confinement camps for American Japanese, fearing that they might provide assistance to Japan during the war. These were acts of bigotry in which innocent people were punished. Write a poem that explores possible reasons for racial or religious discrimination.

References

Listed below are references that were used in writing *Where Did All the Cowboys Go?* The resources were used to confirm dates, verify names of games, tests given, and to validate the author's memory.

Andrew, James H and others, *History and Map of Greene County: Brochure.* Jefferson, IA: Greene County Historical Museum, 2004.

Apps, Jerry. *One –Room Country School: History and Recollections.* Woodruff, Wisconsin: The Guest Cottage Inc., 1996.

Bennett, Herschel and others, *Social Studies, Grades Two through Eight.* Des Moines, IA: Iowa Department of Public Instruction, 1944.

Eighth Grade Examination May 5, 1950, Des Moines Iowa, State of Iowa: Department of Public Instruction. 1950.

Felbinger, Lee. "Cowboys Heroes from the Colorful Past." *Reminisce,* March/April 2004.

Fond Flashbacks 1947, *Reminisce* January/February 2005.

Fond Flashbacks 1946, *Reminisce* May/June 2002.

Fond Flashbacks 1950, *Reminisce* May/June 2001.

Fond Flashbacks 1949, *Reminisce*, March/April 2004.

Fond Flashbacks 1948, *Reminisce*, November/December 2005

Fullenton, Charles A, *New Elementary Music: A One-Book Course.* Chicago IL: Follett Publishing Company, 1936.

Fuller, Wayne. *Old Country School, The Story of Rural Education in the Middle West.* Chicago, IL: University of Chicago Press, 1982.

Fuller, Wayne. *One-Room Schools of the Middle West, An Illustrated History.* Lawrence, Kansas: University Press of Kansas, 1994.

Grove, Myrna J. *Legacy of One-Room Schools.* Morgantown PA: Masthof Press, 2000.

Historic Pages From The Des Moines Register and Tribune, December 8, 1941, July 14, 1942, January 12, 1943, June 6, 1944, April 13, 1945, May 8, 1945, August 6, 1945. August 14, 1945. Des Moines, Iowa: Des Moines Register.

"History: More Towns Greene County, Iowa. Farlin" http://files.usgwarchives.org/ia/greene/history/towns.txt.

Kennedy, David M. *Freedom from Fear: The American People in Depression and War, 1929-1945.* New York: Oxford University Press, 1999.

"Music Test for Eighth Grade Examination." State of Iowa: Spring 1950

Rathburn, Frankie Beathard. *Ten Kids and a Teacher: Memoires from a One Room School*. Enumclaw, WA: Pleasant Word, Division of Wine Press Publishing, 2006.

Sherman, William. Editor, *Iowa Country Schools: Landmarks of Learning*. Parkersburg, IA: Mid-Prairie Book. 1998.

Smith, Nila Banton. *At Home and Away: The Unit-Activity Reading Series*. Chicago: Silver Burdett Company. 1935.

Theobald, Paul. *Call School: Rural Education in the Midwest to 1918*. Carbondale IL: Southern Illinois University Press, 1995.

Thorin, Richard. "When Movies Were Magic." *Reminisce Extra*, March 2000.

Wessels Living History Farm, Ganzel, Bill. "Farming in the 1940s" updated 5/2010 http://www.livinghistoryfarm.org/farminginthe40s/farminginthe1940s.html.

Zimmerman, Jonathan. *Small Wonder: The Little Red Schoolhouse in History and Memory*. New Haven: Yale University Press, (2009).

1941-41 to 1949-50 Bristol Township Teacher Reports to County Superintendents on record at the Prairie Lakes Area Education Agency office in Fort Dodge Iowa. They are now stored at the UNI Museum at the University of Northern Iowa.

1950 Eight Grade Test Results on record at the Prairie Lakes Area Education Agency office in Fort Dodge Iowa. They are now stored at the UNI Museum at the University of Northern Iowa.

Appendix A

Eighth Grade Test Information

The 1950 test was prepared by the Iowa Department of Public Instruction and given to all eighth grade students on May 5, 1950. There were 544 questions measuring the student's knowledge and understanding in reading, arithmetic, language, social studies, science, and health. A separate music test, identified as the *State of Iowa Music Test for Eighth Grade Examination* was also given. The test was a multiple choice test, and there was no writing assessment. Gene correctly answered 402 of the 544 questions and all of the music test questions.

The questions printed here are a sample of the 544 questions and reveal much of what the values and beliefs were at the end of the 1940s.

Reading Questions

There were thirty reading questions with seven reading sections including one on general information, advertisements, a newspaper story regarding the White House, a book review from *Spurs for Suzanna*, an excerpt from a Judy Canova Broadcast radio program, a weather story, and questions interpreting a cartoon. Listed below is the book review from the 1947 book and questions, 24, 25, and 26, that were asked. Following the book review is section 5, which was an excerpt the Judy Canova broadcast and questions 27, 28 and 29.

Section No 4 from Reading Test
Brief Book Review: *Spurs for Suzanna* by Betty Cavanna

Suzanna's father is in the hospital; her mother has a job and selfish Suzanna is feeling sorry for herself because the usual summer vacation at the seashore is impossible. She has always loved horses but has never done any of the chores connected with their care. During her stay with the Ballentine family she gains some new friends and learns the values of work and of consideration for others. She earns her spurs.

24. This book review is
    1) written with too much detail.
    2) written to keep boys from reading the book.
    3) intended to show that the book is shorter than most.
    4) short but gives a good idea of what the book is about. (Correct answer.)

25. This book reviews is written to
    1) tell enough of the story so others will want to read the book. (Correct answer.)
    2) point out that it is a very poor book.
    3) show that girls need to know how to feed and water horses.
    4) suggest that the author was writing on a topic of which she knew little.

26. The writer of this book review has described Suzanna as
    1) a girl with an undesirable quality which never changes.
    2) a girl who has always loved to care for horses.
    3) a girl who earns the right to wear spurs and ride horses. (Correct answer.)
    4) a girl who changes a desirable quality into an undesirable one.

Section No 5
Excerpt from Radio Program: Judy Canova Broadcast

Judy Canova, walking into a dress shop: "I would like to see some silk dresses."

Saleslady, "You wouldn't like a silk dress this time of year, would you? It's much too cold. You should buy one of these lovely new wool dresses. They just came in today."

Judy Canova: "No, I want a silk dress this time. I don't care how cold the weather is! I don't want a wool dress"

Saleslady: "Why are you so insistent? Why do you have to have a silk dress?"

Judy Canova: "I'm getting sick and tired of having the wool pulled over my eyes."

27. Insistent means
    1. rude
    2. clever
    3. determined (Correct answer.)
    4. humorous

28. This section from a radio program is amusing because
    1. Judy Canova does not like to put on or take off wool dresses.
    2. the saleslady is so insistent.
    3. Judy makes use of an expression which has a double meaning. (Correct answer.)
    4. silk dresses should not be worn in the wintertime.

29. The saleslady is
    1. necessary so Judy can get her joke across to the radio listeners. (Correct answer.)
    2. not trying to make a sale.
    3. rather insolent.
    4. a real one.

Arithmetic Questions

There were sixty-two arithmetic questions. The test was divided into four sections: fifteen computation questions, fifteen meaning and fundamental concept questions, fifteen vocabulary and general information questions, and seventeen arithmetic problems to solve. Listed below are sample questions from each of the sections.

Part I - Computation questions 12 and 15.

12. 7/8 x ¾ =
    1) 6 5/8
    2) 5 1/32
    3) 80 ½
    4) 5 21/32
    5) answer not given (Correct answer.)

15. If P = a + b + c. P = 10, a = 4, b = 3 then c =
    1) 3 (Correct answer,)
    2) 17
    3) 7
    4) 14
    5) answer not given

Part II - Meanings and fundamental concepts questions 5 and 12.

5. John had 345 sticks. He tied these sticks into as many bundles of 10 sticks each as possible. Which of these statements would be true about what John did?
   1. It was possible to tie all of the sticks into bundles of 10.
   2. John had 45 bundles of 10 sticks.
   3. John had 34 bundles of 10 sticks. (Correct answer.)
   4. John had 3 bundles of 10 sticks.
   5. None of the answers are correct.

12. Wayne worked a division example and got 2 for an answer. What would the answer have been if he had changed the divisor and dividend around?
    1. 2.
    2. Can't tell without knowing more about the numbers Wayne used.
    3. .05.
    4. ½ (Correct answer.)
    5. None of the above answers is correct.

Part III – Vocabulary and General Information questions 7 and 14.

7. A line intersecting another line at right angles is:
   1. a perpendicular line.9 (Correct answer.)
   2. a parallel line.
   3. an equal line.
   4. an oblique line
   5. answer not given.

14. In a right triangle the line opposite the right angle is:
    1. the base line.
    2. the altitude.
    3. the tangent line.
    4. the hypotenuse. (Correct answer.)
    5. answer not given.

Part IV - Arithmetic problems: number 7, 15, and 17

7. While cultivating corn with a two-row cultivator, a farmer cultivated 80 rows of corn. He knew the rows were a half-mile in length. Approximately how many miles did he travel while cultivating? The choices are:
   1) 40 miles (Correct answer.)
   2) 28 miles
   3) 20 miles
   4) 80 miles
   5) answer not given.

15. Mr. George and Mr. James made a joint profit of $10,000. If this is divided in the ratio of 3 to 5, how much will each receive?
   1) $3,000 and $5,000
   2) $3,750 and $6,250 (Correct answer.)
   3) $4,000 and $6,000
   4) $1,250 and $8,750
   5) answer not given.

17. A play room is 33 feet long and 18 feet wide. What would be the dimensions of a scale drawing of this room if a scale of ¼ inch represents 1 foot?
   1) 8 ¼ in. x 4 ½ in. (Correct answer.)
   2) 24 ¾ in. x 13 7/8 in.
   3) 11 in. x 8 ½ in.
   4) 33 in. x 18 ½ in.
   5) answer not given.

Language Questions

The language test had a total of two-hundred and twenty-three questions. Thirty of them were spelling words, forty-seven were language usage questions, seventy were punctuation questions, and seventy-six were capitalization questions.

Part I - Spelling questions 1, 2, 7, 25, and 24

The spelling exercises provided four words in parentheses. Students were to select the one word in the exercise that is misspelled, and mark it on the answer sheet. If none are misspelled they place a mark in the fifth box on the answer sheet.

Question number 1
1) (Saterday) afternoon (Misspelled)
2) an (original) story
3) a (knowledge) of Latin
4) a good (friend)

Question number 2
1) the (necesity) of water (Misspelled)
2) the (preparation) of food
3) a (scientific) report
4) an old (magazine)

Question number 7
1) a (rural) school
2) a progressive (community)
3) the (ability) to learn
4) a large (purchase) of grain
(No words are misspelled)

Question number 25
   1) a sincere (apology)
   2) an (atheltic) director (Misspelled)
   3) a difference of (opinion)
   4) a (daily) paper

Question number 29
   1) to perform an (experiment)
   2) the (gymnasium) floor
   3) to play in the (orchestra)
   4) to play (rehersal) (Misspelled)

Part II - Usage questions 1, 10, 19, 35, and 37.

Students were to select the correct usage in forty-seven sentences.

Question 1 Where does she keep (1. them at?) or (2. them?) (2 is correct answer.)

Question 10 He has (1. grown) or (2. growed) fancy tomatoes to sell. (1 is correct answer.)

Question 19 It was (1. He) or (2. Him) who showed me how to swim. (1 is correct answer.)

Question 35 (1.Us) or (2.We) boys went down the hill to the creek. (2 is correct answer.)

Question 37 (1.Set) or (2.Sit) beside me, please. (2 is correct answer.)

Part III – Punctuation questions from business letter.

In the punctuation test students were requested to insert the proper punctuation in sentences and in a letter. Below is the letter that they are to proof and insert correct punctuation.

Blake and Sloane Publishing Co
25 S Main Street
Detroit Michigan

Gentleman
Please send me one copy of Tom Sawyer by Mark Twain
I am enclosing a check for three dollars.

>Yours truly
>Roy M Stookes

Part IV – Capitalization questions from a thank you letter.

In the capitalization test students identified the words that should be capitalized in twelve sentences, one poem, and a business letter. Below is the business letter in which they were asked to identify the words that should be capitalized.

>224 north Cedar street
>Storm lake, Iowa
>May 14, 1949

Mr. A. L. Woodstock
Alta, Iowa

dear sir:
    In the name of the student council of whittier school, I wish to thank you for your interesting talk to our student body last friday afternoon. Your talk on "The conservation of wildlife in Iowa" was of great value to us. It was especially so because we live in a lake region and are often tempted to disregard state games laws.
    We wish everyone in buena vista county and even in other counties of Iowa might have heard you.

>sincerely, yours,
>Mark Stevens
>secretary

Joe Millard

Social Studies Questions

There were 154 questions on the social studies test. Following are questions 15, 16, 20, 23, 25, 27, 30, 31, 32, 33, 35, 41, 54, 64, 95, and 105.

Question 15. The constitution of the United States has endured as a suitable instrument of government for more than one hundred and fifty years. Which of the following sentences explains that fact?
1. It was framed by a body of able men.
2. It was put into effect by George Washington.
3. It provides for a flexible government of the people, by the people and for the people. (Correct answer.)
4. It would consume a long time to construct a more suitable instrument.

Question 16. An import is:
1. a tax on articles.
2. an article sent to another country.
3. an article brought in from another country. (Correct answer.)
4. a manufactured article of this country.

Question 20. The main reason that the farm population of Iowa has decreased is that:
1. Farm production has decreased.
2. More and more farm machines are being used. (Correct answer.)
3. The people are no longer eating as much food.
4. Less and less machines are being used.

Question 23. During the past summer the United States approved the:
1. South Pacific Treaty
2. North Atlantic Treaty (Correct answer.)
3. Hudson Bay Treaty
4. Pan-American Treaty

Question 25. The main reason we in the United States fear Communism is that:
1. Communists use violent means to bring about what they want.
2. We do not like the Russians.
3. We could lose our property if the Communist controlled our government.
4. We would lose the freedoms we have so long worked for. (Correct answer.)

Question 27. Northerners who went to the South and tried to use the Negro vote to control the government were known as:
1. Ku Klus Klanners
2. Scalawags, (Correct answer.)
3. Carpetbaggers,
4. Mugwumps.

Question 30. David wanted to be elected president of his class. During the week before election he did the following things. Which one do you think was undemocratic?
1. He told the class what he would do if elected president.
2. He gave a talk in class, asking everyone to vote for him.
3. He told the class he would try to have more parties if elected.
4. He asked the individual members of the class to vote for him because he went to a particular church. (Correct Answer)

Question 31. We think of the United States as the leader of democracy in the world. Of this we are proud. The best way we can show the rest of the world the value of the democratic way of life is to:
1. Let them all know we have more cars, roads, refrigerators and, radios, than any other country.
2. Show the world we have more atomic bombs and a better army than anyone else.
3. Show them what wonderful soil, mines, and other natural resources we have.
4. Prove to the rest of the world that our democratic ideals are being followed here in the United States. (Correct answer)

Question 32. We are fortunate in having many nationalities, religions, and cultures blending in the United States because it results in:
1. Many small divided communities, none bothering the other.
2. Children having the chance to learn many languages.
3. Ideas from all the groups being united to form our American culture. (Correct Answer)
4. All people being allowed to keep their loyalty to their native lands.

Question 33. The airplane was invented:
1. before the Revolutionary War.
2. between the Revolutionary War and the Civil War.
3. between the Civil War and World War I. (Correct answer.)
4. between World War I and World War II.

Question 35. We consider ourselves the best informed nation in the world. A democratic country must have a well-informed people to retain its democracy. The best way o get a correct picture of our national news is to:
1. select one daily newspaper to read and stick to it.
2. listen to the daily news on the radio.

3. make up our own minds on questions and not read a newspaper.
4. read two or more daily newspapers of different points of view. (Correct answer.)

Question 41. The term "ninety per-cent" of parity concerns certain:
1. automobile parts
2. irrigation projects
3. farm products (Correct answer)
4. school taxation

Question 54. The President of the United States is elected by the:
1. Senate.
2. direct popular vote.
3. state legislatures.
4. electors in the states. (Correct answer.)

Question 64. Which of these men does not fit into the group?
1. Da Gama
2. Hudson
3. Cortez
4. Galileo. (Correct answer.)

Question 95. Arabia has recently attracted the attention of the world. Why?
1. an earthquake
2. uranium deposits
3. development in the production of petroleum (Correct answer.)
4. a typhoon

Question 105. Political parties raise their campaign funds by:
1. taxes,
2. selling bonds,
3. Congressional appropriations,
4. contributions by members of the parties. Correct answer.)

Map Questions

On a map of the United States students were asked to identify the following locations.

Iowa, Detroit, The French Quarters, Los Angeles, the most important seaport city, the city noted for manufacturing automobiles, the city with the largest railroad center and is meat packing city, the region noted for livestock ranching and wheat production, the region with the greatest density of population, the most mountainous region and 13 other locations.

Social Studies Vocabulary Words

Students needed to know the meaning of these words.

Irrigation, erosion, prohibition, reconstruction, drought, surplus, tributary, Boycotting, suffrage, rebates, monopoly, intervention, source, legislation, economics, republic, ordinance, delta, toleration, and allies.

Science and Health Questions

There were fifty-five multiple choice questions. Students were told there could be several correct answers but they were to select the *best* answer. There were also fifteen vocabulary words that students were expected to know. Following are questions 1, 10, 12, 20, 22, 25, 27, 32, 46, 47, and 48 selected from the multiple choice questions.

1. A major concern of the dairy farmer is the action of bacteria on milk. Cooling prevents or retards the spoilage caused by the action of bacteria on milk. It is recommended that milk be cooled by circulating water around the can. This is done because it cools the milk more rapidly. It is important to cool milk rapidly because:
    1. the farmer has more time to work in the field.
    2. water is cheap and plentiful on the farm.
    3. it shortens the time during which the bacteria can reproduce. (Correct answer.)
    4. it enables all the dairy to be located in the barn.

10. In an aquarium we have four goldfish, three snails, and green plants. What is likely to happen?
    1. The goldfish will become weak and some will die.
    2. The snails will die.
    3. The plants will grow and flourish.
    4. The situation will remained unchanged. (Correct answer.)

12. John was in the eighth grade and his brother, Bill, was in the sixth grade. Bill got the flu and the doctor prescribed pills to be taken every six hours. After Bill recovered some pills remained. These pills should be:
    1. kept in case John gets the flu.
    2. used only for Bill if he gets sick again.
    3. used only if Bill gets the flu again
    4. destroyed. (Correct answer.)

20. If in a school accident, a child suffered a severed artery in the neck, it would be important to remember to:
  1. bandage the wound.
  2. apply a tourniquet.
  3. locate a first aid kit quickly.
  4. locate the pressure points. (Correct answer.)

22. In order to have food for "off" seasons, man preserves food by canning, drying, or freezing. This prevents the food from spoiling because food preserved in one of these ways:
  1. has had the germs in it killed.
  2. can be easily stored in the cellar.
  3. does not allow bacteria to reproduce. (Correct answer.)
  4. has had the supply of oxygen removed.

25. The following weather conditions were observed on a July day in Sioux City, Iowa: The sky was clear, the barometer was high, the temperature was 75 degrees F; the wind was blowing from the northwest. Which of the following forecasts seems most likely on the basis of these weather conditions?
  1. A rain storm approaching.
  2. Rain is to be expected within 24 to 36 hours.
  3. No change in the weather is expected within in the next 36 to 48 hours. (Correct answer.)
  4. This is typical tornado weather.

27. During the past year, less than five cases of smallpox were reported in Iowa. Control of this disease has been gained by good health practices. Which of the following health practices was used to "stamp out" this disease?
  1. Quarantine.
  2. Immunization. (Correct answer.)
  3. Hygiene.
  4. Health examinations in school.

32. The bag limit on pheasants in Iowa is two cock pheasants. This limit is fewer than the limit allowed a few years ago. The best explanation of this change in bag limit is:
   1. the winters are becoming more severe, and the winter death rate is increasing.
   2. farming practices have reduced natural cover. (Correct answer.)
   3. hay is put up about the time the young are being hatched and the nesting grounds are destroyed.
   4. heavy rains in the spring have "drowned out" the nests.

46. Is this statement a superstition, observed fact, opinion of scientists, or truth arrived at by experiment: For the best yield potatoes should be planted in the light of the moon? (Correct answer is superstition)

47 Is this statement a superstition, observed fact, opinion of scientists, or truth arrived at by experiment: Vaccination is effective in preventing certain diseases? (Correct answer, truth arrived at by experiments.)

48. Is this statement a superstition, observed fact, opinion of scientists, or truth arrived at by experiment: The drinking habit in regard to alcohol is inherited? Correct answer is opinion of scientists)

Science and Health Vocabulary words,

Students were expected to know the meaning of these words: manufacture, environment, inherited, reflect, quarantine, preserves, contaminate, disperse, restoration, larva, nutrition, scientific theory, and bacteria.

Music Test for Eighth Grade Examination

Each question has five possible answers. Choose the answer which best answers the question, and place the number of that answer in the space ahead of the number of the question.

1. An Italian word used in music to indicate that a composition is to be played quickly is
    1. andante,
    2. allegro, (Correct answer.)
    3. largo,
    4. forte,
    5. piano.

2. Ritard (rit.) is an indication to
    1. slow up, (Correct answer.)
    2. speed up,
    3. sing more loudly,
    4. sing more softly,
    5. stop singing entirely.

3. In two-part singing at school, the higher part is generally called
    1. alto,
    2. bass,
    3. soprano, (Correct answer.)
    4. viola,
    5. baritone.

4. What kind of a note receives one-half the time value of a quarter note?
    1. eighth note, (Correct answer.)
    2. quarter note,
    3. sixteenth note,
    4. half note,
    5. dotted half note.

5. What kind of note received one-half the time of a whole note?
    1. quarter note,
    2. eighth note,
    3. sixteenth note,
    4. half note, (Correct answer.)
    5. dotted half note.

6. You can tell how many beats are in a measure by looking at the
    1. clef sign,
    2. key signature,
    3. composer name,
    4. song title,
    5. time signature. (Correct answer.)

7. The letter names of the lines of the treble staff are:
    1. f a c e,
    2. e g b d f, (Correct answer.)
    3. c e a b d,
    4. d g c a g,
    5. a b c d e.

8. In the last three years, the Choir Songs have included a song by the composer Brahms. Its title was
    1. Columbia, Gem of the Ocean,
    2. Dixie Land,
    3. The Little Dustman, (Correct answer.)
    4. Hills of Tyrol
    5. Marianina.

9. In the last two years, the Choir Songs included a song by the composer Schubert. Its title was
    1. The Linden Tree, (Correct answer.)
    2. Hills of Tyrol,
    3. Marianina
    4. Dixie Land,
    5. Slumber Boat.

10. Old Dog Tray, The Glendy Burk, and My Old Kentucky Home are songs composed by one of America's favorite song writers. His name is
   1. W. A. Mozart,
   2. Francis Scott Key,
   3. Stephen Foster, (Correct answer.)
   4. Irving Berlin,
   5. Samuel Ward.

Appendix B

An Iowa High School Admission Certificate was given to Gene to confirm that he had passed the requirements that were needed to be admitted to a high school.

Iowa High School Admission Certificate

This Certifies That GENE MILLARD has shown proficiency in the Common School Branches and is therefore entitled to admission to High School in accordance with the Laws of Iowa, and the regulations of the admitting School.

Given at JEFFERSON, IOWA

GREENE County, Iowa,

this 19 day of May 19 50

No.

R. W. Morris
County Superintendent of Schools

Appendix C

The high achieving rural and nonpublic eighth grade students were awarded a small felt "I" letter to identify them as Honor students. Gene was awarded such a letter. However the author is not certain what criteria were used to award a student an Honor I letter. It is believed that the letter was presented to students who achieved a high test score on the State Eighth Grade Examination, a high score on the State Eighth Grade Music Examination, overall excellent grades, and was recommended by their teacher to receive the award.

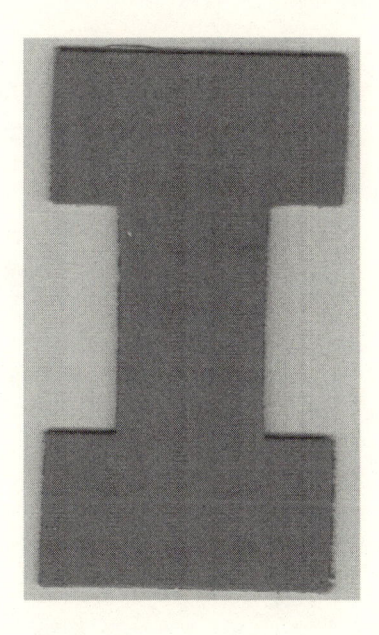